The Model of a Hedonistic Human Being versus the Social Responsibility of Consumers

GRZEGORZ HOPPE

New York 2014

Book reviewed by:

Prof. Tadeusz Borys

Prof. Teresa Słaby

Copyright © Grzegorz Hoppe

All rights reserved.

New York 2014

ISBN: 1493704370

ISBN-13: 978-1493704378

grzegorz.hoppe@op.pl

For Wiesia

Table of Contents

Introduction 7
1. The model of a hedonistic human being 13
   1.1. Hedonism in the history of economic thought 15
   1.2. The role of the unconscious in consumer behavior 19
   1.3. The model of a hedonistic human being – *Homo hedonismus* 23
   1.4. A system of values versus *Homo hedonismus* 36
2. *Homo hedonismus* versus theories of consumer decision-making and consumer choice 41
   2.1. *Homo hedonismus* and the basic laws and hypotheses of the theory of consumption 43
   2.2. *Homo hedonismus* in the context of Tversky and Kahneman's prospect theory and the hyperbolic discount function 49
   2.3. Psychological aspects of information asymmetry 54
3. *Homo hedonismus* and the contemporary psychological concepts of a human being 57
   3.1. Behaviorism 59
   3.2. The psychodynamic approach 63
   3.3. The cognitive approach 67
4. The socialization process and consumer decisions 71
   4.1. The influence of religion on consumer behavior 73
   4.2. The influence of culture on consumer behavior 84
   4.3. Sensory deprivation vs consumer choices 99
5. Verifying the model of a hedonistic human being by means of a research experiment 103
6. The model of *Homo hedonismus* in management science 113
   6.1. The importance of the model of a hedonistic human being in management science 115
   6.2. Three dimensions of social responsibility 117
7. The basics of the development of responsible consumer behavior 121

	7.1.	The impact of a society's affluence on the level of responsible consumption... 124
	7.2.	Determinants of the growing level of socially responsible consumer behaviors 126
	7.3.	A model of socially responsible consumer decisions 132
8.	Consumer social responsibility – ConSR 139
	8.1.	Consumer social responsibility in the CSR system............................ 144
	8.2.	ConSR vs sustainable development 148
	8.3.	The influence of information asymmetry on the level of ConSR .. 153
	8.4.	The role of the state in creating socially responsible consumer behavior... 154
	8.5.	Research problems related to ConSR – the mind-behavior gap..... 158
	8.6.	Measuring the level of ConSR – the results of own research........... 164
9.	Prospects for the development of ConSR 189
Summary 194
References 198
Annex 1 206
Abstract... 214

THE MODEL OF A HEDONISTIC HUMAN BEING VERSUS THE SOCIAL RESPONSIBILITY OF CONSUMERS

Economy is the art of making the most of life.

George B. Shaw

Introduction

The social sciences, such as management science or psychology, are currently multiparadigmatic [Kozielecki 2000; Sułkowski 2012], which is a result of at least two phenomena. First, most theories that were developed as part of these sciences have little predictive power, which can be understandable in the context of the evolution of humankind. The two past centuries in particular saw tremendous changes in the development of human behavior, which was related to rapid economic, scientific and technological progress. Second, there are many scientific theories that have been formulated by researchers in each of the above-mentioned fields of science and there are no leading theories that the majority would be willing to accept. The nature of the human being is one such unresolved issue. *Homo economicus* is still the most popular model in economics and management science although it has long since been heavily criticized for not reflecting real human nature. However, no better concept has been developed to date and, therefore, it is still assumed that this model is adequate. On the other hand, the two Nobel Prizes in Economic Sciences that were awarded in 2001 and 2002 have been the most significant examples of rejecting the idea of a human being as one making rational economic decisions. Joseph Stiglitz, Michael Spence, George Akerlof, Vernon Smith and Daniel Kahneman were granted this prize for research in the area of consumer behavior under conditions of uncertainty or information asymmetry, among others. They proved that people are neither rational nor objective and that their choices are largely guided by emotions and subjectivity. As for psychology, it is an even more complicated area of research because there are more equally important conceptions of humankind. These are mainly behavioral, psychodynamic, and cognitive theories. The differences between them are so large that none of them has managed to gain recognition among these competing theories as yet. At the same time each theory uses certain elements of other theories that are recognized by most researchers. It seems that one might draw eclectically on these concepts, but such a solution is not accepted at present.

I have decided to make an attempt to reconcile the existing paradigms by introducing my own axiomatic model of a human being. The concept of axiomatics is associated with mathematics, and the very idea behind this project was to apply one of the principles of the natural sciences to the social sciences. Axioms are primary, undeniable truths which do not have to be proven. And that should be the case for this model – it will either be accepted by the world of science as corresponding to reality or it will be fully challenged. The new model of a human being that is proposed here is not entirely new, at least as far as historical approaches to human nature are concerned, but, to this day, it has not been presented in the literature as a uniform concept. The basic assumption of the model is that a human being is a hedonist by nature, hence its name: The Axiomatic Model of a Hedonistic Human Being (abbreviated as AMHHB) or *Homo hedonismus*. The correct process of determining the rules that govern human nature should, by definition, be highly predictive in character given, for example, the time that is needed for the evolutionary development of humankind and, consequently, for changes in a human being's nature.

The way in which people make decisions, especially consumer decisions, and why they behave in a certain manner are important issues that are addressed by all economic theories, but they primarily constitute the main topics that are investigated by management science and, in particular, are compatible with the behavioral approach to management. Arriving at answers to which no one would raise objections would have great significance, in particular to the many applicable solutions used in organizational theory. This model can be used in such subfields as strategic marketing, consumer relationship management or consumer decisions.

The main aim of this book is to:

introduce the Axiomatic Model of a Hedonistic Human Being that would present actual consumer behavior

This aim has been achieved by carrying out the following research tasks:

- checking if the Axiomatic Model of a Hedonistic Human Being is consistent with selected economic theories
- checking if the AMHHB is consistent with contemporary psychological conceptions of humankind
- establishing what influence the socialization process has on changes in consumer behavior given the adopted AMHHB
- establishing what the consequences of introducing AMHHB are on the social responsibility of consumers (ConSR)
- determining the scenario of ConSR's development in accordance with the adopted model of a human being

The following hypotheses were put forward in this book:

H1: The Axiomatic Model of a Hedonistic Human Being correctly reflects the real nature of human behavior

H2: AMHHB is consistent with the economic theories of consumer

behavior

H3: AMHHB is consistent with the eclecticism of contemporary psychological conceptions of humankind, in particular with commonly accepted theories

This model of a hedonistic human being is not the only possible representation of human nature; it is merely an attempt to create a concept that would prove useful in describing consumer behavior. It is a model that is assumed to be descriptive and serves the purpose of describing consumers' behavior and choices in the most realistic manner possible. However, it certainly does not provide a complete picture of a human being, whose nature is much more complex. It is worth noting that the model does not take into account, for example, such psychological phenomena as feelings. Nonetheless, in my opinion, the model's generality, assumptions and reductionist character make it possible to both develop and verify consumer theories.

The model of a hedonistic human being that is introduced here is of vital significance for shaping social responsibility in all of its dimensions. It is particularly important for making it possible to develop the social responsibility of consumers. Responsible consumption is an issue which is currently widely being described, especially in relation to such concepts as sustainable development, corporate social responsibility or degradation of the natural environment. Building a high-level ConSR worldwide would be of considerable importance for all of these areas. However, the question arises as to how a human being becomes a socially responsible person and what can stimulate the development of socially responsible behaviors in the context of the adopted model of human nature.

This book also attempts to provide answers to the above-mentioned problems. In the first part of this book I analyze changes in the approach to human nature in the history of economic thought, introduce the axiomatic concept of *Homo hedonismus* and present verification of its consistency with the most important theories in economics and management science related to the theory of consumption. Then an analysis of contemporary psychological conceptions of humankind is presented in the context of the proposed image of human nature.

Based on the proposed axiomatics of the theory of *Homo hedonismus* this part of the book presents a discussion of the influence of religion and culture on consumer choices and social behaviors. It also introduces the issue of the social responsibility of consumers.

The following parts present verification of the model by means of a research experiment, a description of the importance of the model of *Homo hedonismus* for management science, an analysis of ConSR's influence on issues related to CSR and sustainable development as well as an analysis of the influence that information asymmetry has on ConSR and a discussion of the possible activities that the state could carry out in order to develop ConSR. The last part of this book deals with the issue of the intention-behavior gap in research on ConSR and an analysis of a survey of the level of ConSR – the results of which additionally confirm the proposed hypotheses – as well as an analysis of the prospects for ConSR's global development.

The book also presents a specific discussion of an issue which has not been resolved to this day, i.e. who truly rules the economy – consumers or businesses. These voices in the discussion are represented by the views of two great figures in economics.

John Kenneth Galbraith (1908-2006) claimed that it is not the sovereign consumer (the alleged "king of the market") but the producer who decides what to produce. He believed that businesses implement a system for exerting social pressure on consumers, mainly through highly developed marketing engineering. Producers not only manufacture a given product, but they mainly create a need for this product in society, i.e. consumer demand, usually before it is launched. He wrote that a consumer who is not fully sovereign fully becomes a puppet in the producer's hands.

Ludwig von Mises (1881-1973) was of a different opinion. In his view, consumers have a significant and often underestimated impact on the dynamics of market processes, which is why – from the perspective of neoclassical economics – it is they who are the real "masters" of a market economy and who decide which businesses are to survive and which are to disappear by making consumer choices [von Mises 2008, p. 43].

Here the question then arises of whether consumers decide on their own what their object of desire will be and whether they determine the utility of goods themselves or succumb to manipulation by businesses. The economic reality is that very often even the best advertising cannot promote goods that are not accepted by society. On the other hand, ideas of new products are oftentimes first generated solely by businesses and there is no real demand for such products at the planning stage.

It is of crucial importance for any further reflections that this problem be solved. If Galbraith is right then there is no such thing as responsible consumption or the social responsibility of consumers (ConSR) – everything is decided upon by businesses and it is only corporate social responsibility (CSR) that should be considered. However, if one assumes that it is von Mises who is right, then both the responsibility of businesses and that of consumers are valid.

CHAPTER ONE

*

The model of a hedonistic human being

Hedonism in the history of economic thought (1.1)

The nature of human actions and consumer choices has been debated in economics from the very beginning of this science. Even the father of modern economics, Adam Smith (1723-1790), who had a background in philosophy, wrote in his book titled *The Theory of Moral Sentiments* (published in 1759) that human economic behavior is based on two human psychophysical characteristics:

- a tendency to be vain, greedy and lazy; and
- a tendency to divide work (specialization).

Smith perceived a human being as an egoist who only aims to have the greatest amount of goods in order to satisfy all of his or her needs while putting in the smallest amount of work possible. People engage in altruistic behavior only when they themselves can benefit from an action that does good to someone else. However, he believes that it is a human being's egoistic attitude that brings benefits to other people and hence to society as a whole. It can generally be stated that a human being is an **egoist** by nature according to Adam Smith's economic theory.

Jean Baptiste Say (1769-1832) followed Adam Smith in his liberal views in France. His major work, *A Treatise on Political Economy; or the Production, Distribution, and Consumption of Wealth* (published in 1803) presented, among others, a new approach to the value and prices of goods. Say believed that it is the purchaser's and the producer's **subjective perception** of **a good's utility** that is a decisive factor in determining both its price and value. He also considered the cost of manufacturing a given product to be its minimum utility and, at the same time, its minimum value. While the assertion about the minimum utility (value) should be disregarded, as it is not true, it should be noted that the idea of the subjective perception of a good's utility is reflected in the theory of exchange, which is valid to this day and which defines exchange as subjectively non-equivalent.

Say's utility theory of value gave rise to another direction in economics – marginalism which is also called the subjective or psychological trend of thought in economics. This trend was developed by Jeremy Bentham (1748-1832), an English economist who was also the founder of the school of thought which has been referred to as utilitarianism. According to utilitarianism, a human being is guided in his or her actions by **the hedonistic principle of utility** which leads to benefits, pleasure and happiness. In his fundamental work titled *An Introduction to the Principles of Morals and Legislation* (published in 1789), Bentham questions the objectivity of social and economic rules. In his opinion, all human behavior is governed by only two factors, namely pleasure and pain, which are the most important motives behind people's actions. Bentham believed that **the principle of utility**, understood in this way, **is an axiom of economics** that does not need to be proven. Utility is based on two concepts, i.e. pain and pleasure, which are measurable and comparable. What can be measured is their value, which depends on the intensity of pleasure and pain, their duration, certainty of occurrence and temporal proximity.

The marginalist, or marginalist and psychological, approach to economics was founded on Bentham's theory. The German economist and statistician Herman Gossen (1810-1858) was the forerunner of this trend in Europe. When formulating his theories he assumed that the main motivation behind human behavior is to achieve the highest level of fulfillment of one's needs, i.e. satisfaction and pleasure. He is currently most known for the two laws he formulated, i.e. the saturation of wants and diminishing marginal utility. The marginalist and psychological trend developed simultaneously as part of several schools of economic thought, and among the most well-known representatives of this approach are:

- Carl Menger (1840-1921), Eugen von Böhm-Bawerk (1851-1914) and Friedrich von Wieser (1851-1926) – the Austrian School;
- Alfred Marshall (1842-1924), John Bates Clark (1847-1938) and William Stanley Jevons (1835-1882) – the Anglo-American School, also called neoclassical economics;
- Leon Walras (1834-1910) and Vilfredo Pareto (1848-1923) – the Lausanne School.

W. S. Jevons had similar views to those of Bentham; he believed that the fulfillment of consumers' needs should be a key economic issue, whereas pleasure and pain are the basic components of economic calculation. Jevons claimed that economics should answer the question how one can achieve maximum satisfaction of needs with minimal effort, i.e. achieve maximum pleasure while experiencing minimal pain. He also dealt with the topic of utility and pointed to the common mistake of confusing the concepts of total utility and marginal utility. Moreover, he rejected the possibility of the existence of a good's objective value based on work. One of his important postulates was that the future (potential) value in use should be included in economic analysis, which led to having the time factor be taken into account. A consumer should consider both the current and future utility of goods in order to implement the postulate of maximizing their utility. Jevons believed that the value of any good is reflected in the following:

- utility value, i.e. a good's total utility
- intensity of desires, i.e. marginal utility
- exchange ratio, i.e. exchange value (price).

Vilfredo Pareto replaced the analysis of marginal utility with an indifference curve and the theory of consumer choice. Indifference curves connect points at which combinations of two goods give an equal level of satisfaction to a consumer. Pareto claimed that it was impossible to combine the subjective utility of goods with quantitative methods, which translated into analyses of consumers' preferences in the form of the consumer **preference curves** that he proposed. He introduced the concept of **ofelimity** (*ophelimite*), which meant 'the level of satisfaction' or 'a consumer's satisfaction with a purchased good'. The development of marginalist-psychological economics ended at the beginning of the twentieth century. Currently there is still a small group of economists who follow this school of thought, but their views are not dominant in today's economics. This approach, however, has formed the basis of most contemporary economic trends. This overview of selected directions in the history of economics shows that the assumption about a human being's hedonistic nature has already been made many times before. It seems, however, that – as humankind – we have not yet been able to acknowledge our hedonistic nature, and this is why such a conception is not part of mainstream economics today. The subsequent chapters of this book will present an attempt to convince the reader that it is time that the concept of *Homo hedonismus* be reintroduced to economics and management science.

The role of the unconscious in consumer behavior (1.2)

Sigmund Freud (1856-1939) claimed that a human being is a hedonist by nature. This is how people are born, and they are consciously or unconsciously guided by the pursuit of delight. Freud, the father of the psychodynamic concept of the human being, pointed out in his research that people are mostly guided by drives and instincts, whereas our unconscious subordinates all our decisions to the need to regulate the ratio between pleasure and the lack of pleasure [Freud [1915] 2009, p. 114]. Even if our consciousness, which develops throughout our lifespan, is seemingly governed by other objectives, it is at a level of the unconscious where decision-making processes take place which lead one to satisfy his or her drives. This does not mean that people are no different from animals and are unconditionally governed by drives and instincts only. Human consciousness (ego), which is understood as a psychological state in which one is aware of both internal (thoughts) and external (the surroundings) phenomena, based on which he or she makes decisions, is influenced by the environment and undergoes changes in the course of one's life as part of the socialization process. It is mostly shaped by culture, religion, upbringing, and education. This does not mean that we cease to be hedonists, but, at the very most, that our consciousness, when influenced by the environment, overcomes drives in certain situations and we can then take other factors into consideration. However, even empathetic or altruistic behavior is most often motivated by a desire to achieve purely hedonistic long-term goals. We are often able to give up immediate pleasure in order to receive even more of it later.

The effect of being guided by drives and instincts is most easily observed in infants. A newly born human being only seeks to satisfy his or her needs. In this period of life, i.e. when the consciousness is not yet fully developed and when the environment has not left its imprint yet, one can most clearly see that hedonism is inherent in people's primordial nature. All messages sent by infants signal that they want to satisfy one of their needs. Because they do not have their own consciousness yet, one may state that this is how the unconscious works and that this is what humankind's nature is like.

As for consumer behavior, one of the laws in economic theory very accurately portrays human nature, namely *the law of subjectively non-equivalent exchange* [Balicki 2002, p. 64]. This law describes the nature of the decision-making process behind an exchange during which people seek to achieve maximum benefit, as subjectively perceived, through an act of exchange. The greater the subjective benefit, the more we are willing to exchange something for something else.

The unconscious is also the sphere where human habits are formed. As research shows, as many as 40% of daily human activities do not result from conscious decisions, but from habits. What we order to eat, how we speak, whether we economize or spend all the money we have earned, whether we do sports and how often as well as how we think and how we work – these are all habits that are of great importance to the health, efficiency, financial security and happiness of every human being [Duhigg 2012, p. 20]. It has been found that, from a biological perspective, habits are formed in the deeper layers of the brain, where the evolutionarily older and more primitive structures are located; these are responsible for automatic behaviors such as breathing, swallowing or experiencing fear. Habits are located more in the center of the brain, i.e. in oval cell structures called the basal ganglia [Duhigg 2012, p. 42].

The habit formation process takes the form of a three-part loop (Fig. 1.2.1):

- First, there is a cue – or trigger – that tells the brain to go into automatic mode and prompts it to start a particular habit.
- Then there is routine, which can have a physical, mental or emotional character.
- At the end of the loop there is a reward, which is important for recording information in the brain saying that a given behavior (habit) is worth remembering.

After a habit has been formed, the brain ceases to consciously participate in making decisions and everything begins to take place in the unconscious. Habit formation is an incredibly important process for a human being because if it did not occur, people would not be able to think creatively and would only be occupied with carrying out basic life functions.

On the other hand, habits are action maps which are encoded in the unconscious and which are based on the cue-reward (benefit, pleasure) pattern. This means that these are purely hedonistic behaviors.

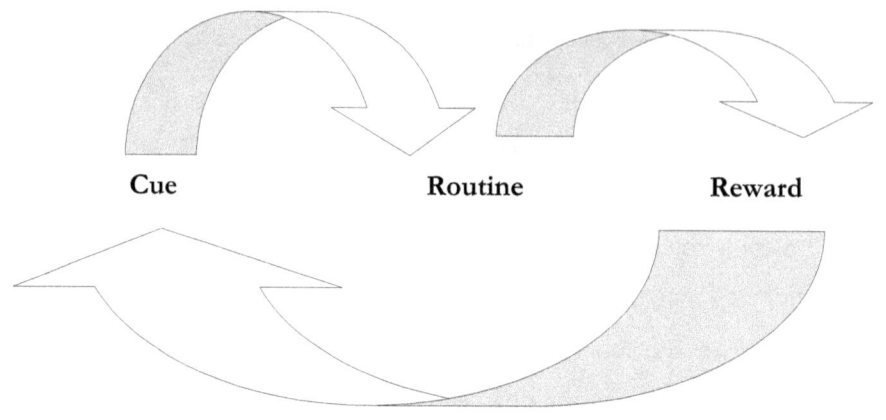

The habit loop

Fig. 1.2.1. The habit loop.

Source: Own work based on Duhigg 2012, p. 49.

Therefore, based on research studies concerning the nature of habits, it can be concluded that habits are responsible for as many as 40% of behaviors, are hedonistic in character and are located in the unconscious. This information is important to studies on consumer behavior because it means that many of the choices people make have the nature of habits and hence are incredibly difficult to change. Currently, the marketing departments of many companies take advantage of this fact – they know how habits are developed and try to create advertisements that will lead to the unconscious formation of desirable habits in consumers. Here the question arises about who decides what choices consumers make – is it the businesses with their large teams of marketing specialists that stimulate the formation of habits or is it that habits are only formed when consumers first consciously accept a given product and want to get hold of it? In order to answer these questions one must first determine the true and real nature of a human being.

The model of a hedonistic human being – *Homo hedonismus* (1.3)

> *They [Cyrenaics] assert that some people may fail to choose pleasure because their minds are perverted;*
>
> Diogenes Laertius

A human being has been portrayed by economic scientists for over 150 years as making rational economic decisions. The concept of a rational human being who makes choices in such a way as to obtain maximum utility, i.e. *Homo economicus*, was introduced to economic theory by John Stuart Mill[1] in the nineteenth century. However, the concept has been heavily criticized and rejected by many economists as inconsistent with reality, in particular with respect to assumptions about people's rationality and objectivity. Contemporary economics, which increasingly more often deals with issues of consumption, is shifting its focus from the traditional representation of a human being as *Homo economicus* to *Homo consumens*. Nowadays, the importance of psychology, sociology and culture is growing as far as studies on economic phenomena are concerned. Psychology plays a particularly significant role in describing human behavior. The issue of consumers' choices constitutes a very important issue in economics, but it

---

[1] *Essays on Some Unsettled Questions of Political Economy*, published in 1844.

is the development of psychology that has brought many new theories explaining such processes. The growing knowledge on how the human brain is constructed and how it works has become a starting point for the development of new research directions aimed at explaining consumer behavior. This is visible, for example, in the fact that the psychologist Daniel Kahneman won the Nobel Prize in Economic Sciences in 2002. The issue of consumption and consumer choices has become an interdisciplinary topic.

As economics developed, many new conceptions of a human being were also formulated: *Homo economicus, Homo consumens,* or the recently developed *Homo sustinens*. Economists have been trying to prove that human nature is compatible with the above-mentioned concepts, but it turns out that none of these conceptions has survived the test of time and none of them reflects the real human nature. In order to fill in the existing gap in the research, I propose that we introduce the concept of *Homo hedonismus*, i.e. a hedonistic human being. The idea of perceiving human nature in this way is not new, as was shown in the preceding section. This time, however, I propose that this conception be introduced axiomatically and that it also be related to the most important economic theories as well as to contemporary psychological conceptions of a human being.

Before presenting the proposed axiomatics, it would be worthwhile to take a look at how the term 'hedonism' is defined in the dictionaries and encyclopedias. This is important because the idea of human nature that is presented here is linguistically consistent with both socially and historically accepted descriptions of the concept of hedonism.

According to the online dictionary of English, *Oxford Dictionaries*, the word 'hedonism' means:

- the pursuit of pleasure; sensual self-indulgence

- the ethical theory that pleasure (in the sense of the satisfaction of desires) is the highest good and proper aim of human life.

The free encyclopedia, *Wikipedia* (Polish version) defines 'hedonism' in the following way:

Hedonism (Greek: ἡδονή, *hedone*, 'pleasure', 'delight') – a view, or a doctrine, according to which pleasure, or delight, is the highest good, the aim of one's life and the main motive behind human actions. The avoidance of pain and suffering is the main condition for achieving happiness.

One may distinguish between:

- ethical hedonism
- psychological hedonism
- materialistic hedonism (hedonistic materialism, consumerism).

The term 'ethical hedonism' refers to the view that people should aim to achieve happiness (for others or for themselves) because it is "ethically good".

According to psychological hedonism, people desire happiness, but nothing is said about how to achieve it (or what kind of happiness it should be).

Materialistic hedonism is the idea that the accumulation and consumption of material goods is the highest or the only value.

Cyrenaic hedonism is the oldest form of this school of thought. It can be characterized as follows:

- What matters is only one's "personal" happiness, i.e. so-called individual hedonism (the experiences of other people are unknowable).
- One can achieve happiness through momentary pleasures.

- What we call "long-term happiness" is the preponderance of pleasure over pain.
- Happiness is "active", i.e. it is an active state of mind, spirit or soul, and it does not mean a lack of suffering.
- It is the current experiences that are important. It does not matter what was or what will be.
- Delight must be harmonized with reason, which means that it is not the human being that is to give in to delight, but that delight is to give in to the human being. Pleasure is perfect when it can be experienced without regret or pain.

Hedonism was advanced by the representatives of a philosophical school that was founded in the fourth century BC by Socrates's student, Aristippus of Cyrene. Later the doctrine of hedonism became distorted and the school ceased to exist in the third century BC.

Given the above-mentioned definitions and in order to be consistent with them it is proposed that the nature of a hedonistic human being be presented axiomatically:

The axioms of a hedonistic human being's nature (*Homo hedonismus*):

1. ***Homo hedonismus* seeks to achieve subjective pleasure, or a benefit, and to achieve its maximum amount, as subjectively perceived.**
2. ***Homo hedonismus* has both a short-term and a long-term aversion to risk – it is a fear of the risk of not obtaining pleasure, or a benefit, or the fear of experiencing something unpleasant.**

3. *Homo hedonismus* chooses between immediate pleasure, or a benefit, and pleasure, or a benefit, to be obtained in the long term so as to maximize it.
4. Every *Homo hedonismus* might individually arrive at his or her own subjective definition of pleasure and a benefit, which may change during his or her lifetime due to the influence of his/her environment.
5. Every action of *Homo hedonismus* is determined by the functioning of both the unconscious and consciousness, with the unconscious processes having priority over the conscious ones when it comes to choosing a given behavior.
6. *Homo hedonismus*'s unconscious is always oriented toward achieving pleasure, or a benefit, while his or her consciousness is shaped throughout his/her lifespan by the environment, i.e. by culture, religion, moral and legal principles, upbringing as well as science, and this is why *Homo hedonismus* may take on attitudes other than hedonism.
7. *Homo hedonismus*'s unconscious is mostly shaped by drives and instincts (in particular by the sex drive, which causes the unconscious to seek sexual pleasure).

The above axiomatics must be presented in more detail and explained so as to avoid unwanted interpretations and for the sake of clarity. Therefore, the text below contains an interpretation of each of the axioms and examples in order to better illustrate each topic.

Homo hedonismus seeks to achieve subjective pleasure, or a benefit, and to achieve its maximum amount, as subjectively

perceived – this means that, generally speaking, every human being directs all of his or her actions toward obtaining pleasure (a benefit). The word 'subjective' emphasizes the fact that every person perceives and experiences various feelings and material benefits in a different way. Both a physical sensation and a psychological experience can be pleasurable, for example, sexual intercourse, having one's favorite meal, listening to music or receiving an award at work. Benefits are also perceived in various, subjective ways; for one person, getting a luxury car will be the greatest benefit, while for another this will be a trip around the world, and for yet another obtaining an academic degree will be the greatest benefit. For some people the fact that they have a finer house than their neighbor, as subjectively perceived, will be a source of pleasure. Maximization of pleasure is also a subjective matter and it depends on what pleasures and benefits one prefers. It should be added that this axiom also includes altruistic behavior. It is not difficult to imagine that there are people for whom doing good to others is the greatest pleasure. Is it not that the altruistic behavior that can often be observed among the very wealthy results from the fact that they have already obtained all the other pleasures and benefits? Is this not a purely hedonistic attitude? Is it not that such behavior gives those people pleasure and brings them benefits? It seems that, having observed the behavior of many people who first achieved financial success and then engaged in charitable activities, one can easily answer these questions in the affirmative.

Homo hedonismus **has both a short-term and a long-term aversion to risk – this is a fear of the risk of not obtaining pleasure, or a benefit, or the fear of experiencing something unpleasant** – this means that the urge to minimize all kinds of risk is an important element of human nature. People do not behave rationally, i.e. they do not objectively optimize their actions, nor do they take the opportunity to obtain the potentially greatest benefit if it is fraught with a risk that is not acceptable to them from their subjective point of view. Subjective perception of the probability of an event taking place, which is usually not a mathematical probability, is also an important aspect of this axiom. *Homo hedonismus* evaluates events whose probability of occurrence is medium and high differently from events whose probability of occurrence is low, i.e. he or she underestimates the likelihood of the former happening and overestimates the likelihood of the latter. What is also important is an event's distance in time – negative events that are to happen in a very remote future are usually underestimated and the probability of their occurrence is insignificant. Such an approach means greater risk aversion when it is possible that negative events might happen in the near future, also when the probability of their occurrence is low; as well as a low risk aversion when it is possible that negative events might happen in a distant future. For instance, many people engage in unhealthy behavior that gives them momentary, subjectively perceived pleasure, for example, they drink alcohol, smoke cigarettes, or have casual relationships, the negative consequences of which are underestimated, i.e. people subjectively perceive the probability of their occurrence as lower than it truly is. On the other hand, when we buy a lotto ticket we make plans for what we could do with the money for a couple of days until the draw – we overestimate the likelihood of a benefit. Even if we are well prepared for an exam we estimate our chances of success to be lower than one would reasonably expect, and we believe that it is likely that we might lose a job the next day even if there is no good reason to think so. The tendency described in the last example also leads people to save a part of their income; in order to avoid the unpleasant experience of having a reduced standard of living in the future, which is a manifestation of our aversion to the risk of losing income in the future, we allocate a portion of our income for future consumption.

Homo hedonismus **chooses between immediate pleasure, or a benefit, and pleasure, or a benefit, to be obtained in the long term so as to maximize it** – this means that people distribute pleasure, or a benefit, rationally – in their opinion – so as to make it last as long as possible and so that its total value is the highest, as subjectively perceived. People are able to give up part or all of a pleasure (benefit) at the present moment if they are convinced that this will bring them greater benefits; for instance, they distribute consumption over time instead of spending all of their income immediately after a desire for a given pleasure has appeared if such a pleasure could lead to unpleasant experiences in the immediate future, for example, such as not being able to satisfy one's basic, physiological needs. A *Homo hedonismus* is also able to endure some unpleasantness at present if this might lead to the possibility of obtaining greater pleasure in the future. Such a choice is, however, only possible if the total subjectively expected value of a pleasure is higher than it would be if the person had not experienced any unpleasant things in the beginning. For example, people will not purchase a thing they desire at the present moment that is unpleasant for them, in order to buy another thing in the future if they desire it even more than the former and if they might derive greater satisfaction from obtaining the latter. Is it not that we often decide not to acquire many products if we do not desire them very much in order to save a larger sum of money and fulfill our real dreams?

Every *Homo hedonismus* might individually arrive at his or her own subjective definition of pleasure and benefit, which may change during his or her lifetime due to the influence of his/her environment – this means that everyone is different and perceives pleasure and benefit differently, which is why we desire different goods and non-material values. This situation is reflected in people's different tastes in both material (e.g. they buy different car brands) and non-material (e.g. they listen to different kinds of music) things. This axiom also indicates that the environment has an influence on changes in human nature during one's lifetime. What is pleasurable, or beneficial, at the beginning of one's life does not have to be so, and usually is not, at its end. Such changes also occur as people gain social status and education or become wealthier. Also, the culture and religion of the society in which a given person functions have a significant impact on the way he or she defines pleasure (benefit).

Every action of *Homo hedonismus* is determined by the functioning of both the unconscious and consciousness, with the unconscious processes having priority over the conscious ones when it comes to choosing a given behavior – this means that, according to Freud's theory and current psychological knowledge, people's actions are determined by the processes that take place in their unconscious and by those that occur in the consciousness. Unconscious processes are primordial and they are mostly based on instincts and drives. Such processes occur beyond our sensory perceptions and do not enter our consciousness. It is these processes, however, that are most often responsible for our final decisions and choices. If it was not for the unconscious, it is very likely that highly developed societies would be doomed for extinction. If people did not have a sex drive, then conscious acts of procreation would occur increasingly less often in such societies. A human being cannot change the principle that has been adopted as part of this axiom in any rational and natural way.

***Homo hedonismus*'s unconscious is always oriented toward achieving pleasure, or a benefit, while his or her consciousness is shaped throughout his/her lifespan by the environment, i.e. by culture, religion, moral and legal principles, upbringing as well as science, and this is why *Homo hedonismus* may take on attitudes other than hedonism** – this means that the subconscious is always directed toward obtaining pleasure (benefit) and wants to obtain it at once, and it has a purely hedonistic character. Consciousness, which is influenced by the unconscious, develops throughout one's lifespan and changes under the impact of various elements of the environment. Among the most important factors that shape the consciousness are: a given society's culture, religion and moral customs. The influence that the environment has on one's consciousness may cause certain decision-making processes that take place there to be other than hedonistic in character. As for human nature, such decisions will mean an unpleasant experience (or at least a lack of pleasure), which people will only accept because of the strong influence of the environment.

***Homo hedonismus*'s unconscious is mostly shaped by drives and instincts (in particular by the sex drive, which causes the unconscious to seek sexual pleasure)** – this means that we unconsciously mainly seek to satisfy our drives and instincts. The sex drive is particularly strong, which causes people to obtain sexual satisfaction even against the moral standards and ethical principles that are generally accepted in a given society. This drive is so strong that a human being can succumb to it even if it might have negative consequences. This is how, for example, two people may enter into a relationship that is based on casual sexual intercourse and is not a considered decision. The drive may also lead to an unintended unpleasant experience, both at once and in the future; for example, one might become infected with a sexually transmitted disease.

Such axiomatics of a hedonistic human being's nature seems to be the most consistent with the reality we observe and it may accurately describe people's behavior in different economic conditions. It is very likely that many people's first reaction will be to say that we are not simply only hedonistic; our consciousness is not willing to acknowledge that this is truly our nature. We often proclaim that we adhere to noble principles in life, that we are altruists, share with others and help them, etc. We are not, however, able to admit that everything we do for others we, in fact, do for our own satisfaction, for our own benefit.

From an ontological perspective, *Homo hedonismus* is a primordial entity which has been described by means of certain accepted axioms, and these are changeless and unambiguous. As for epistemology, however, one should study, get to know and describe *Homo hedonismus* as well as his or her behavior through the prism of the main principle that people adhere to, i.e. of pursuing pleasure, or a benefit, and avoiding unpleasantness. One should study every behavior, action and choice of a human being, understood in accordance with the proposed model, by focusing on a human being's pursuit of pleasure, or a benefit, and aversion to the risk of experiencing unpleasantness and to potential unpleasantness. Among the benefits are: subjectively obtained utility and satisfaction from having certain goods or non-material values, while any deterioration from the baseline state means unpleasantness. A lack of changes in the baseline level of one's satisfaction is also perceived as unpleasantness when the level of satisfaction of people in one's immediate vicinity is rising. It should also be noted that scientific methods (methods of description) that are employed for the purpose of such a model of a human being are axiological in character. This means that it would be very difficult to use a mathematical apparatus to describe *Homo hedonismus*, except for comparative aspects, such as "bigger and smaller".

The model that has been adopted for the purpose of this book certainly does not reflect the entirety of human nature, but it has been adapted for its intended function, namely to serve as a basis for formulating theories and hypotheses in management science and economics.

The words of the famous Israeli writer, Amos Oz, also bear testimony to the true nature of a human being: "People should not be in the business of working harder than they should be working… In order that they get more money than they need. In order to buy things they don't want… In order to impress people they don't really like."

Additionally, one cannot disregard the very important assumption that this model of human nature only applies to healthy people, or more specifically, to mentally healthy people. Maslow expressed a similar view in reference to hedonism: "Hedonistic theory does work for healthy people; it does *not* work for sick people…" [Maslow 1998, p. 52]. He also excluded the mentally ill from the group of people to whom this theory applies. If one accepts Maslow's statement, this will logically lead to the assertion that people who are not aware of their hedonistic nature are probably mentally ill. This is also what Cyrenaics claimed, as can be concluded from the sentence cited at the beginning of this section.

The accepted level of reductionism and generality is another important assumption of the model that is described in this book. The model portrays consumers' attitudes that are consistent with reality, and this is what it has been created for. To avoid misunderstandings, it should be clearly stated that this model does not provide a full description of the human psyche or of all possible emotional states; in particular, it does not deal with such psychological phenomena as feelings. Therefore, it is not a model of a human being but of human nature and it only describes the sphere of consumers' decisions and choices.

It should be added that this model of *Homo hedonismus* does not refer to a human being who does not have a system of values; it does not describe a simple human being who is only driven by animal impulses and or a blind pursuit of any kind of pleasure. The next section presents the conception of a hedonistic human being and, additionally, explores the topic of people's values in life.

A system of values versus *Homo hedonismus* (1.4)

The concept of a hedonistic human being shows what factors we take into consideration when making choices concerning various matters. Every person has a hierarchy of needs indicating the order in which they should be satisfied. Such a hierarchy is usually referred to in the literature as a system of values. According to this hierarchy, first the lowest-order values (needs) are fulfilled and then, after the lowest needs have been met, higher-order values (needs) are fulfilled. Max Scheler (1874-1928) was one of the philosophers who dealt with these issues; his ideas have been used until today; Karol Wojtyła (later Pope John Paul II), among others, took up Scheler's thought. As part of an *a priori*, timeless, transhistorical and objective hierarchy, Scheler identified five types of values:

- religious (the divine and the holy)
- spiritual (pure knowledge of the truth as well as of what is beautiful, or esthetic, and righteous)
- vitality-related (related to life and death, and to what is noble)
- hedonistic (what is pleasurable)
- utilitarian, civilization-related (useful).

These values make up an eternal hierarchy, with religious values being higher than the other values. A lower-order value is subordinated to a higher-order value (utilitarian values are needed so that hedonistic values can be fulfilled, whereas hedonistic values are subordinated to the vitality-related ones, etc.); on the other hand, each higher-level value provides a rationale for the existence of a lower-order value (money is meaningless if it cannot give one pleasure, and experiencing pleasure makes no sense if it does not boost our vitality; life has a meaning when one devotes him- or herself to an idea, etc.). Religious values, i.e. divinity and holiness, are also understood directly and intuitively, but they relate to objective reality [Hostyński 1998]. According to Tomaszewski [1984], values perform specific functions in the process of a human being's individual and social development, namely:

- Values regulate the way in which one satisfies his or her needs. Needs define what is important for an individual's life and proper functioning, whereas values determine needs and establish the way in which they are to be satisfied. Moreover, values make it possible for an individual to decide which needs are to be met and in what order.
- Values have an impact on one's long-term goals and the ways in which these are achieved, i.e. on one's life plans.
- Values influence one's self-esteem, for example, the way in which a given person evaluates his or her appearance and abilities as well as interpersonal relationships. These values have an impact on how people assess the results of their actions and, consequently, on whether they are satisfied or not satisfied with their achievements.

The adopted model of a hedonistic human being assumes that everyone also has his or her own system of values which is created in the process of socialization; it is slightly different from the one presented by Scheler, yet it fulfills the functions that have been proposed by Tomaszewski. A system of values is shaped in the process of socialization and it changes over time, which usually causes the hierarchy of values to become modified as it develops (matures). In particular, higher-order values gain significance. In my opinion, the system of values which derives from Scheler's hierarchy takes the following form in the model of a hedonistic human being:

- metaphysical values (related to the essence of being)
- spiritual values (esthetic, cognitive and related to the legal order)
- vitality-related values (related to life and death as well as health and security)
- utilitarian values (utility-related)

In this system, religious values have been replaced with metaphysical values and, most of all, hedonistic values have been removed. Each of the above-mentioned values corresponds to human hedonism in this system, which means that all of them are fulfilled based on the basic principle of hedonism, i.e. the pursuit of pleasure, or a benefit, and the avoidance of unpleasantness. Here, hedonism is understood as the essence of human nature and not as a value. In order to fulfill any of these values, a human being acts in such a way as to achieve pleasure (benefit), and has a natural aversion to the risk of experiencing unpleasant things (Fig. 1.4.1).

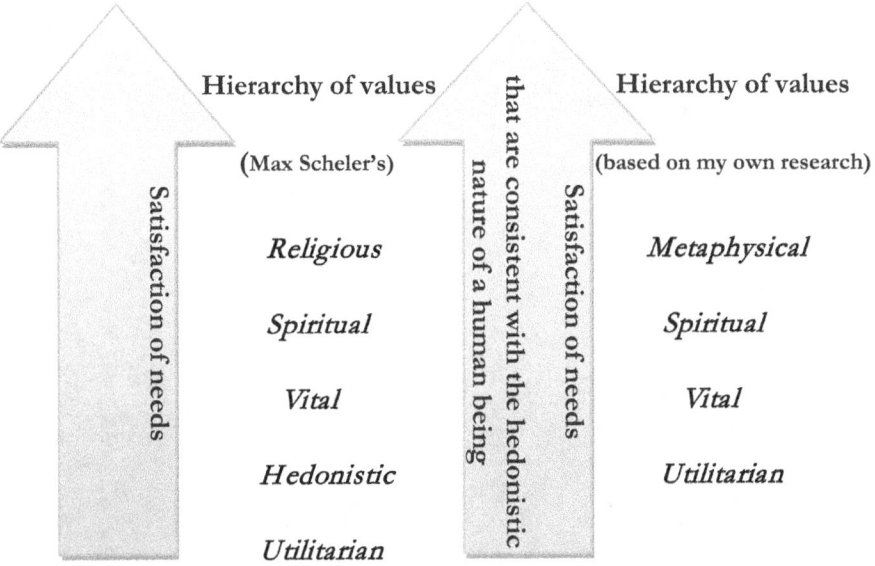

Fig. 1.4.1. Hierarchy of values according to Max Scheler and my own, modified hierarchy of values.

Source: Own work.

In order to establish whether the adopted concept of a hedonistic human being is consistent with reality, the following sections will analyze its consistency with selected economic theories as well as with psychological conceptions of humankind.

Chapter Two

*

Homo hedonismus versus theories of consumer decision-making and consumer choice

Homo hedonismus and the basic laws and hypotheses of the theory of consumption (2.1)

The concept of a hedonistic human being mostly refers to human nature with regard to issues related to consumer decisions. Over the past several centuries many laws concerning demand, decision-making processes and the theory of exchange have been formulated. The text below presents an analysis of the most predictive theories in the context of the proposed concept of *Homo hedonismus*.

- **Hermann H. Gossen's law of diminishing utility:**

As the consumption of a given commodity grows, the rate of increase in satisfaction with each subsequently acquired unit of this commodity becomes smaller.

Consumers seek to distribute their income in such a way that every unit of money spent on the last unit of every good they have purchased yields the same increase in utility (satisfaction).

Gossen's law is subjective in character and is entirely consistent with the first axiom of a hedonistic human being, i.e. the one which states that *Homo hedonismu*s seeks to achieve subjective pleasure, or a benefit, and to achieve its maximum amount, as subjectively perceived. This law is almost identical to the above-mentioned axiom and this fact does not have to be supported with additional arguments.

- **Ernst Engel's law:**

As income grows, the proportion of expenditure on food to total consumption expenditure falls.

Ernst Engel's law is also entirely consistent with the first axiom of a hedonistic human being, i.e. the one according to which *Homo hedonismus* seeks to achieve subjective pleasure, or a benefit, and to achieve its maximum amount, as subjectively perceived. This axiom clearly indicates that, having satisfied his or her physiological needs, a hedonistic human being will not be spending increasingly more income on subsequent food products as that would lead to a failure in maximizing pleasure (satisfaction). Certainly, as one's income rises, one may change his or her consumption habits with regard to food and start buying higher-quality or healthier products, or one may start using food services to an increasing extent instead of preparing meals at home. This, however, does not change the fact that the proportion of expenditure on food to total expenditure will fall and that we cannot indefinitely increase the amount of food products we consume for biological reasons.

- **John M. Keynes's absolute income hypothesis:**

As income increases, consumption also increases but at a lower rate.

John M. Keynes's absolute income hypothesis is compatible with the second and third axiom of a hedonistic human being, which state that *Homo hedonismus* has both a short-term and a long-term aversion to risk – it is a fear of the risk of not obtaining pleasure, or a benefit, or the fear of experiencing something unpleasant; and that *Homo hedonismus* chooses between immediate pleasure, or a benefit, and pleasure, or a benefit, to be obtained in the long term so as to maximize it. This is how, according to

Keynes's law, a hedonistic human being behaves – he or she does not spend all of his or her additional income because of both an aversion to risk and an inclination to distribute pleasure over time. Due to an aversion to the risk of an income decrease in the future, people save a part of their income in order to be able to use it later. This is definitely a manifestation of fear that an unpleasant experience might occur in the future, which is minimized by lowering the rate of consumption.

- **Milton Friedman's permanent income hypothesis**

The level of consumption expenditure does not depend on current disposable income, but on long-term, past and average permanent income.

Milton Friedman's permanent income hypothesis is compatible with the second and third axiom of a hedonistic human being, which state that *Homo hedonismus* has both a short-term and a long-term aversion to risk – it is a fear of the risk of not obtaining pleasure, or benefit, or the fear of experiencing something unpleasant; and that *Homo hedonismus* chooses between immediate pleasure, or a benefit, and pleasure, or a benefit, to be obtained in the long term so as to maximize it. This hypothesis is a specific elaboration of the one formulated by Keynes. In this context, all of the arguments that have been presented with regard to that hypothesis also apply to this one. It is difficult to conclude from axiomatics only that the level of spending will result from the average, long-term and past income. This has not been proven for the whole of society with respect to Friedman's hypothesis either. It seems that it would be more consistent with reality and at the same time entirely compatible with the adopted axiomatics if one assumed that this level is subjective and is a result of both past experiences and expectations about the future.

- **The Veblen paradox**

For high-income social groups, a higher price for some goods causes demand for these goods to grow.

This paradox concerns snobbish behavior and is considered anomalous in classical economics. As for the adopted model of a hedonistic human being, such behavior is natural as it results from the desire to obtain a benefit, or pleasure, in the form of a psychological advantage over those who cannot afford such goods. This can now be widely observed not only in groups of very wealthy consumers; for example, there is great demand for Apple products that are much more expensive than their counterparts from other manufacturers.

- **Franco Modigliani and Albert Ando's life-cycle hypothesis:**

The level and structure of consumption expenditure depend on the average past income, current disposable income and the expected future income until the end of one's lifetime.

Franco Modigliani and Albert Ando's life-cycle hypothesis is compatible with the second and third axiom of a hedonistic human being, which say that *Homo hedonismus* has both a short-term and a long-term aversion to risk – it is a fear of the risk of not obtaining pleasure, or benefit, or the fear of experiencing something unpleasant; and that *Homo hedonismus* chooses between immediate pleasure, or a benefit, and pleasure, or a benefit, to be obtained in the long term so as to maximize it. This hypothesis is another elaboration of the two previous ones. Therefore, all of the previous findings are valid, and in particular the assertion that the level of consumption will be based on the subjective perception of this level in the past and subjective expectations about the future level of income. It should be added that the question of subjectivity is of crucial importance here as we are usually not able to precisely estimate (calculate) the level of our past income or to objectively establish the level of our future income.

- **James S. Duesenberry's relative income and the irreversibility of consumption hypothesis**

An individual's level of satisfaction from consumption depends to a large extent on the consumption level of others in his or her surroundings, in particular the social group he or she unconsciously or consciously follows. The level of one's satisfaction from consumption depends on the level of consumption of the group he or she copies. If the consumption level of other people in a given person's environment is higher than his or hers, this person's level of satisfaction from consumption will decrease (imitation effect).

As income rises, consumption expenditure increases too, whereas when consumers' incomes fall, they will try to retain the previous level of consumption (irreversibility of consumption or the ratchet effect)

James S. Duesenberry's relative income and the irreversibility of consumption hypothesis are compatible with the first, second and third axioms of a hedonistic human being, which state that *Homo hedonismus* seeks to achieve subjective pleasure, or a benefit, and to achieve its maximum amount, as subjectively perceived; that *Homo hedonismus* has both a short-term and a long-term aversion to risk – it is a fear of the risk of not obtaining pleasure, or a benefit, or the fear of experiencing something unpleasant; and that *Homo hedonismus* chooses between immediate pleasure, or a benefit, and pleasure, or a benefit, to be obtained in the long term so as to maximize it.

Homo hedonismus's nature makes an individual experience unpleasantness when his or her consumption level is relatively low as compared to the consumption level of people in that individual's environment, regardless of his or her level of consumption measured in objective terms. The same unpleasant feeling occurs when one has to lower his or her consumption level. A hedonistic human being's experiences that are triggered in this way are consistent with the analyzed hypotheses.

It should be added that only the most important axioms of the concept of *Homo hedonismus* that are consistent with the cited theories have been selected, but, in fact, all of the presented laws and hypotheses are compatible with each of the axioms in the theory on *Homo hedonismus*. Given this consistency, one may state that the proposed concept of human nature is compatible with all of the above-mentioned laws and hypotheses concerning the theory of consumption and that it is an accurate reflection of actual human nature.

Homo hedonismus in the context of Tversky and Kahneman's prospect theory and the hyperbolic discount function (2.2)

Amos Tversky and Daniel Kahneman, who did not agree with the rational choice theory, conducted observations of human behavior in relation to perceptions of utility. Based on these studies they concluded that a human being attaches much more importance to the losses he or she has incurred than to the benefit he or she has gained. They stated that losses and gains are perceived asymmetrically, in contrast to the accepted model of rational choice, according to which these are equal values. On the basis of their own research and the results they obtained, they formulated the prospect theory [Tversky and Kahneman 1979, 1986, 1991]. In general, it can be stated that they found that people have a natural loss aversion.

Prospect theory can be defined as follows:
For people, utility does not depend on the overall level of their economic well-being but is relative. The baseline level of utility does not matter, and any worsening of the situation is perceived as a loss and, conversely, any improvement of the situation as a gain. People are sensitive to changes in their situation irrespective of the initial state. A worsening of one's situation will be perceived as being of higher magnitude (a greater loss) than an improvement in it (a smaller gain), although their magnitude will be the same.

Prospect theory means that consumers will perceive a decrease, even a small one, in their income as a significant loss, or unpleasantness, regardless of their current income situation, i.e. even if their level of disposable income is high. The same is true when it comes to an increase in income, which is perceived as a benefit, or pleasure. A very important aspect of this theory is that it has established that the identical values of a worsening and an improvement in one's income situation are not symmetrical, and that a decrease in income is seen as being of much larger magnitude. A very important conclusion has been derived from this theory with regard to human behavior and decision-making, i.e. one that can be formulated as follows:

People by nature seek to increase utility, but they also have a natural loss aversion, which implies that if there is a possibility of improvement which is, however, fraught with risk of loss, they usually give up this opportunity for fear of experiencing a potential loss.

Any loss, even a small one, is perceived as a large decrease in utility, in contrast to a gain of the same magnitude which leads to a very small increase in utility. It should also be noted that there is not much difference between small and large improvements as regards the subjective perception of a benefit. Another conclusion drawn from prospect theory is that for people it is the very change in utility that is of greatest importance, while the size of such change is not that important. This dependence is illustrated in Figure 2.2.1. Tversky and Kahneman also established that, under conditions of risk, people erroneously estimate the probability of the occurrence of events — they underestimate average and high probabilities and they overestimate low probabilities. This leads them to assign decision weights that are too high to events when the real risk of loss or probability of profit is negligible.

Prospect theory is of vital significance for the discussion of human nature as, on the one hand, it challenges the rational choice theory which the idea of *Homo economicus* is based on and, on the other hand, it is consistent with the adopted axioms of the concept of *Homo hedonismus*. Therefore, in fact, it is another theory that confirms that the concept of a human being which has been adopted here is correct. Moreover, the fact that Daniel Kahneman was awarded the Nobel Prize in Economic Sciences for the research that has been presented above is not insignificant – it further confirms that the model of human nature which is perceived in such a way is highly rated by the world of science.

Richard Thaler and Hersh Shefrin were the authors of another important research study into human nature. They found that consumers have two faces: one is rational and far-sighted and the other is purely hedonistic and impatient. These two sides of human nature are in a kind of decision fight, i.e. they choose between gaining immediate benefits and implementing plans as well as providing for benefits in the future [Thaler and Sherfin 1981]. This property of decision-making is called the hyperbolic discount function (Fig. 2.2.2). It is different from an exponential discount function which represents changes in utility over time in accordance with the rational choice theory because the highest discount rate occurs in the first time periods [Loewenstein and Prelec 1992]. As for consumers' decisions, this means that a choice made at the present time has higher utility than a choice made in the nearest future, which often causes the present decisions of consumers to destroy their plans for the future. This property of human nature is also consistent with the model of *Homo hedonismus*, which has been confirmed by the results of an analysis made by the researchers themselves.

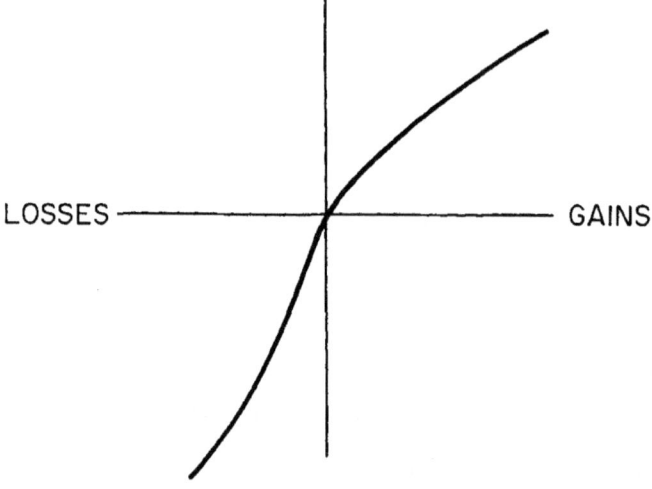

Fig. 2.2.1. Asymmetric utility function.

Source: Tversky and Kahneman 1991, p. 1040.

The chart above shows that a change in utility is much larger under the "losses", which means that the value of a loss is subjectively perceived as representing a bigger change in utility (decline) when compared to a change in utility (increase) for the same value of a gain. Such a way of perceiving gains and losses by consumers causes it to be presented as a subjective, asymmetric utility function.

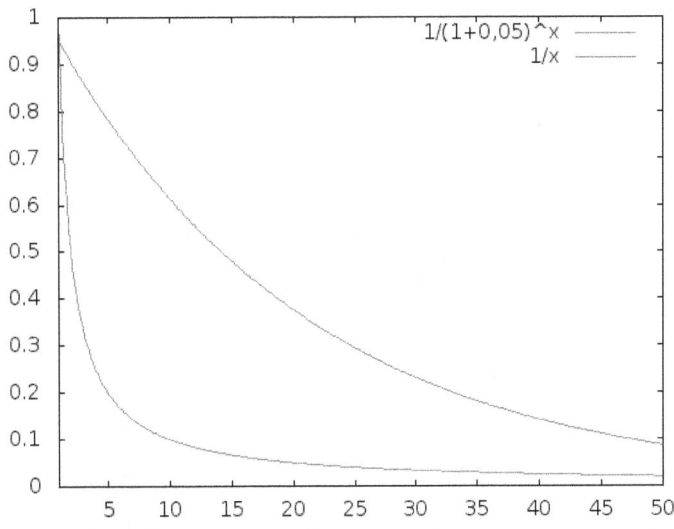

Fig. 2.2.2. Hyperbolic discount function (1/x) and the exponential discount function, a 5-percent discount rate.

Source: Own work.

The example of a discount function as presented in Figure 2.2.2 shows an exponential discount function representing a change in value over time at a five-percent discount rate, i.e. $y = 1/(1+0.05)^x$, which is a real mathematical discount (rational values) at the assumed five-percent discount rate; and a hyperbolic discount function of the $y = 1/x$ type, which corresponds to the subjective way in which consumers perceive a discounted value in relation to time.

The X axis in the chart represents time and the Y axis shows a discount factor. An analysis of both of these functions clearly shows that the first period is the most important because that is when the difference between the real and subjective discount is the largest. This is often used by banks that employ marketing psychology and offer deferment of loan payments to clients thus encouraging them to take out a loan.

Psychological aspects of information asymmetry (2.3)

The issue of information asymmetry has been studied and described by three contemporary economists: George Akerlof, Michael Spence, and Joseph Stiglitz, who received the Nobel Prize in Economic Sciences for their theories in 2001.

This topic was first explored by George Akerlof in 1970. In his article he discussed the issue of the market of used cars and the fact that sellers and buyers have completely different knowledge of such cars. Akerlof pointed out that sellers who know much more about the quality of the cars they offer have an advantage over consumers and can sell cars of below average market quality [Akerlof 1970]. He suggested that this asymmetry could be eliminated by, for example, issuing guarantees that would safeguard consumers' interests. Akerlof's idea was taken up by Michael Spence [1973] and Joseph Stiglitz [1975]. Rothschild and Stiglitz [1976] provided an interesting example of information asymmetry, i.e. the insurance market, where consumers have some information advantage over insurers. A consumer knows the potential risk of a given insurance event taking place, while an insurer only knows the average probability of such an event happening in a particular population.

Information asymmetry is a common phenomenon, and not just in economic life. From a psychological perspective it is related to making decisions based on a certain amount of available information or to taking on additional work in order to obtain more information. In each case a consumer ponders whether it is worthwhile to make the extra effort (unpleasantness) and gain additional information or if he or she should make a decision based on the available information. This problem is solved in accordance with a customer's subjective belief that either his or her choice will meet his or her expectations about the utility level (pleasure, satisfaction) without additional information or that it will be worthwhile to make the effort to search for information (cost, unpleasantness) because doing so will lead to a particular increase in the utility of his or her choice (gain, pleasure).

In general, it can be stated that all markets are characterized by information asymmetry, which causes those markets' participants to have different kinds of information at their disposal and makes them unable to make the most rational decisions possible. It is typical of each of the markets described above that none of their actors has complete knowledge and that information asymmetry exists. In markets operating in this way it is impossible for any of the parties to make choices that would lead to objective maximization of utility, which is in contradiction to the concept of *Homo economicus* and at the same time in accord with the concept of *Homo hedonismus*, according to which a human being seeks the highest subjective utility.

Contemporary economic life is full of information asymmetry, but is it not simply a manifestation of a hedonistic attitude? Is this not how sellers want to obtain more utility from an exchange?

One can ask why the producers themselves do not aim to provide complete information about the goods they manufacture. Is it because many of such goods do not truly possess the advertised properties or because a huge part of production has been moved to regions where child labor is used or where workers are paid less than a living wage?

All of the theories and hypotheses that have been presented in this chapter describe anomalies in the economy. One should, however, think whether these anomalies represent the real nature of human behavior and that all the assumptions about human nature that have been made so far only make up a normative theory which should be revised. When one adopts the proposed axiomatics of the *Homo hedonismus* theory it turns out that this is what the majority of human behaviors are like. I put forward the hypothesis that if one assumes that the concept of *Homo hedonismus* reflects real human nature, which is not a new idea, then this might lead to a better and fuller explanation of many economic issues, especially those which are dealt with by management science, as consumer behavior is a key problem in theories of management. This assumption would also be very important as far as human resources management and relationship management are concerned.

CHAPTER THREE

*

Homo hedonismus and the contemporary psychological concepts of a human being

Like many social sciences, psychology has not developed one, uniform theory and it is multiparadigmatic, which translates into a multitude of psychological conceptions of the human being. Each of these contemporary theories contains laws that are accepted by most researchers in the field, but such laws constitute only a small portion of the theories, which are largely mutually disjointed or exclusive. Because there is no one leading theory, an attempt was made to analyze those that are most often recognized in terms of their consistency with the introduced model of *Homo hedonismus*. This logical construct is to help in finding an answer to the question about the extent to which the concept of a hedonistic human being is consistent with contemporary psychological approaches. As it will be shown in the next sections, the concept of a hedonistic human being ideally corresponds to the eclecticism of all these theories. There exist also other concepts of a human being apart from the ones that are presented here, but the concepts here are the most common. This book does not provide their full description, but it points to the most important achievements related to the theories or those of their elements that concern human nature and consumer behavior.

Behaviorism (3.1)

It is assumed that Burrhus Frederic Skinner (1904-1990) is the father of modern behaviorism. He severely criticized the image of an autonomous human being and created behavioral theory according to which every action that people carry out is dependent on certain genetic traits and, most of all, on the state of the social and physical environment in which they function.

The structure of behavior is to a large extent a copy of the structure of the environment [Kozielecki 2000, p. 24]. Positive and negative reinforcements are the main driving force behind human actions. In simplified terms they can be called rewards and punishments, however, one should remember that they have a broader meaning. Every person may understand the terms 'reward' and 'punishment' differently, as these concepts develop in each person in an individual way in the process of socialization. All human actions are driven by the desire for positive reinforcement and the avoidance of negative reinforcement, i.e. for receiving rewards and avoiding punishments. This part of behaviorist theory does not cause much controversy; however, Skinner also claimed that human consciousness, thought processes and character do not influence people's reactions, which has aroused much controversy among scientists. From this description a picture emerges of an externally controlled human being. The behaviorists assert that it is possible to control human behavior by means of positive and negative reinforcements. Based on many experiments they proved that it is primarily positive reinforcement that leads to a permanent change in human behavior. As for negative reinforcement (punitive control), they proved that one may control people's actions by using such methods, but this will not lead to permanent changes and will only result in avoidance of this kind of reinforcement. It is also worth noting that positive reinforcements, including their strength and frequency, must be adapted to a particular situation and social group if they are to have the expected effect on human behavior. The above is one of the most important findings of behaviorism and it has not been challenged by representatives of other trends in psychology. A vital message emerges from this conclusion, i.e. that real and permanent changes in human behavior can only be achieved by using positive reinforcement. Unfortunately, one may get the impression that no one else, apart from the scientists, is interested in the laws that govern human behavior. The world we live in has been based on the illusory power of punishment throughout its history. All legal systems and a majority of the educational ones regard punitive control as the most effective. Leaving aside the ethical aspects of punishment, such a rationale is a complete anachronism which does not have the slightest chance of changing undesirable human behavior permanently. Negative reinforcement, i.e. broadly defined punishment, usually fails to eliminate asocial behavior as it only dampens and suppresses it temporarily [Kozielecki 2000, p. 45]. In this regard, the administrations of all countries are still stuck in the Middle Ages.

Here it is worthwhile to, once again, postulate that attempts should be made to create social life with only the necessary amount of punishments and which would mostly be based on a system of rewards that would lead to the development of desirable social behaviors. Such a world would be compatible with human nature and with knowledge on human behavior.

Behaviorism is a theory that is consistent with mainstream economics in which, for example, a positive correlation was long since established between positive reinforcement and labor productivity. A system of rewards is widely used in contemporary marketing as well as advertising and for building positive, long-lasting relationships with customers. A comparison between ideas related to behaviorist theory with the concept of *Homo hedonismus* shows that these conceptions are consistent with one another with regard to positive and negative reinforcement, and partly contradictory with respect to external control. The concept of a hedonistic human being assumes that people make decisions autonomously and on the basis of the *subjectively* perceived probability of obtaining a benefit or avoiding punishment. It is an undeniable fact that people are also in a way governed by their environment, but it is people's individual and subjective expectations and predictions concerning the consequences of particular decisions as well as drives that ultimately regulate the decision-making process. The axioms of the *Homo hedonismus* theory that are consistent with behaviorism are primarily the following:

- *Homo hedonismus* seeks to achieve subjective pleasure, or a benefit, and to achieve its maximum amount, as subjectively perceived.
- *Homo hedonismus* has both a short-term and a long-term aversion to risk – it is a fear of the risk of not obtaining pleasure, or a benefit, or the fear of experiencing something unpleasant.

Therefore, the first of the psychological conceptions of humankind that is discussed here is in accord with the concept of hedonistic human nature with respect to aspects that are accepted by most psychologists.

The psychodynamic approach (3.2)

The psychodynamic theory of a human being was formulated by Sigmund Freud (1856-1939) and then elaborated by his successors. Many elements of Freud's theory have been challenged, but its main assumptions have remained unchanged and his theory continues to develop and gain new followers. This conception assumes that human actions are caused by inner motivational forces which very often are in conflict with one another and which are, as a rule, unconscious. Among the motivational forces are mainly drives and needs. The fact that people are unconscious of these forces is the cornerstone of the psychodynamic approach – this is why people very often do not know why they behave the way they do.

Freud's legacy lives on in the form of such propositions as the existence of unconscious motives, the idea of defense mechanisms and the assertion that the first years of life have a decisive influence on the formation of human personality [Kozielecki 2000, p. 98].

Psychoanalysts, i.e. proponents of the psychodynamic approach, distinguish between two kinds of drives: primary and secondary. Primary drives, also known as inborn drives, are the following:

- a desire to get food,
- a desire to maintain optimum body temperature,
- the sex drive,
- avoidance of pain,
- a need for receiving stimuli and contacts with the external world [Kozielecki 2000, p. 101].

Secondary drives come into existence in the socialization process; there are very many of them, for example, the need for security and interpersonal contacts, and personal needs, such as the need for prestige, recognition or power.

Defense mechanisms play a very important role in this theory – these mechanisms to a certain extent protect a person's "self" from fear, guilt, hopelessness or emotional disorders. The most important among them are: repression, rationalization, projection, and substitution. Defense mechanisms act like habits – they allow a human being to cope with a conflict situation, are unconscious and develop in the process of socialization.

Repression is about removing from one's consciousness thoughts about failure, conflict as well as drives and feelings that evoke fear or guilt; it should be distinguished from suppression, which is a conscious reaction. Projection is a mechanism whereby one ascribes his or her own undesirable attributes to others in order to reduce the fear of admitting that he or she is acting in a socially unacceptable manner. The rule is that "if others are like that too, then I am not doing anything wrong". However, this comes down to unconsciously assigning other people characteristics that they do not truly have. Rationalization is another defense mechanism in which people come up with untrue or incomplete motives behind their actions. This is a kind of "moral cleansing" of the motives behind one's behavior before one's environment. People usually declare that they are doing something for others, or for the common good, etc., while their real motivation is purely hedonistic. Substitution is the last of the mechanisms that are presented here and it takes on two forms, namely of compensation and sublimation. Compensation is about directing one's activity toward achieving goals that are similar to those which one was not able to achieve or which one fears. This mechanism might lead to very positive changes; for example, a student may turn his or her failure in sports into success in science. Sublimation is the transformation of one's failures into creative imagination and the world of fantasy. It can also lead to socially positive changes; for example, this is how one's creative abilities can develop. The overview of defense mechanisms shows that their formation is very often caused by hedonistic behaviors that are negatively perceived by society. A person who does not want to admit to him- or herself or to the people in his or her surroundings that he or she is behaving in a hedonistic way creates the mechanism of repression or rationalization.

Psychoanalysts point to the current issue of consumerism. They believe that this phenomenon is also a kind of mechanism defending one against fear. Consumption is a means of avoiding unpleasantness and protecting oneself from, for example, loneliness or the lack of love, or of fulfilling the need to increase one's prestige or self-esteem.

When analyzing the psychodynamic approach, one can state that it is largely consistent with all of the axioms of the theory of *Homo hedonismus*, i.e. the following:

- *Homo hedonismus* seeks to achieve subjective pleasure, or a benefit, and to achieve its maximum amount, as subjectively perceived.
- *Homo hedonismus* has both a short-term and a long-term aversion to risk – it is a fear of the risk of not obtaining pleasure, or a benefit, or the fear of experiencing something unpleasant.
- *Homo hedonismus* chooses between immediate pleasure, or a benefit, and pleasure, or a benefit, to be obtained in the long term so as to maximize it.
- Every *Homo hedonismus* might individually arrive at his or her own subjective definition of pleasure and a benefit, which may change during his or her lifetime due to the influence of his/her environment.

- Every action of *Homo hedonismus* is determined by the functioning of both the unconscious and consciousness, with the unconscious processes having priority over the conscious ones when it comes to choosing a given behavior.
- *Homo hedonismus*'s unconscious is always oriented toward achieving pleasure, or a benefit, while his or her consciousness is shaped throughout his/her lifespan by the environment, i.e. by culture, religion, moral and legal principles, upbringing as well as science, and this is why *Homo hedonismus* may take on attitudes other than hedonism.
- *Homo hedonismus*'s unconscious is mostly shaped by drives and instincts (in particular by the sex drive, which causes the unconscious to seek sexual pleasure).

In addition, it should be emphasized that the defense mechanisms that have been identified by psychoanalysts are definitely an example of hedonistic behavior, which is most often used to justify the way we act.

The cognitive approach (3.3)

Cognitive theory was a response of contemporary psychologists such as J. S. Bruner, H. A. Simon (1916-2001), U. Neisser (1928-2012), D. E. Rumelhart, and T. Tomaszewski (1910-2000) to behaviorism and to the psychodynamic approach, which these psychologists did not agree with. According to this theory a human being is not controlled by the external environment nor is he or she a slave to unconscious motivations and drives, but a human being is rather a conscious entity who independently decides his or her fate and who usually controls his or her behavior in a conscious and purposeful way. The central object of research in the cognitive approach is the cognitive system, which is also called a reproductive-generative system and which has relatively stable properties that have not changed since ancient times. These are: intelligence, special abilities, both remote and recent memory, abstract and creative thinking, language competences, the speed of information processing, etc. These properties are essentially innate, but they develop in the process of socialization [Kozielecki 2000, pp. 170-171]. However, it should be added that the human cognitive system has its limitations and can be fallible. As has been proven by Simon, the bounded rationality of a human being, which is not even close to being objective, is a specific kind of limitation [Simon 1957]. One should mention that the theory of bounded rationality is widely used in economic sciences and is consistent with the concept of *Homo hedonismus*, in particular with these axioms:
- *Homo hedonismus* seeks to achieve subjective pleasure, or a benefit, and to achieve its maximum amount, as subjectively perceived.

- *Homo hedonismus* has both a short-term and a long-term aversion to risk – it is a fear of the risk of not obtaining pleasure, or a benefit, or the fear of experiencing something unpleasant.

The cognitive approach assumes that every human being's system of values is formed in his or her cognitive structures and may change during the socialization process. Cognitive psychology distinguishes between two types of valence: positive valence, which is characteristic of such experiences as pleasure, delight, and curiosity that are sought by an individual, and negative valence, which is typical of negative, adverse experiences such as unpleasantness, fear, and hate – which one avoids.

The above-mentioned assumptions of the cognitive approach are consistent with the following axioms of the *Homo hedonismus* theory:

- *Homo hedonismus* seeks to achieve subjective pleasure, or a benefit, and to achieve its maximum amount, as subjectively perceived.
- *Homo hedonismus* has both a short-term and a long-term aversion to risk – it is a fear of the risk of not obtaining pleasure, or a benefit, or the fear of experiencing something unpleasant.
- *Homo hedonismus* chooses between immediate pleasure, or a benefit, and pleasure, or a benefit, to be obtained in the long term so as to maximize it.
- Every *Homo hedonismus* might individually arrive at his or her own subjective definition of pleasure and a benefit, which may change during his or her lifetime due to the influence of his/her environment.

Studies on and observations of human behavior show that people have different hierarchies of values, both with regard to material goods and spiritual experiences. This has led to the identification of several categories of people based on their preferences for specific hierarchies of values, of which the most important are the following:

- Dionysian values – these are cherished by people for whom the most important are goods such as consumption, comfort or a convenient life, and who pursue a life that will be full of joy and satisfaction. Such people believe that one should make the most of this world and use the gifts of modern industrial civilization to the fullest. Life will be meaningful only when we manage to achieve the things and gadgets we desire as well as luxury, and when we immerse ourselves in consumption-like abundance.
- Heraclean values – by accepting them a human being seeks dominance over others and wants to gain power and fame. Comfort and convenience are not important; what matters is only control over one's environment as well as over social groups and structures. The question of how to gain power and recognition permeates every thought of such a person.
- Promethean values – these add much sparkle and warmth to one's daily life. One who holds such values perceives him- or herself as a part of the community and often engages in altruistic and prosocial behavior. The fight against suffering, evil, cruelty or repression is of the highest personal value for such an individual.
- Apollonian values – people who have these values attach the greatest importance to creativeness, to getting to know the world as well as to the development of science and art. Historically, this was quite an elitist hierarchy, as only "those whom the gods love" dealt with art and science. It can be expected that in the future this creative attitude and innovative lifestyle will prevail and that a human being will find the meaning of his or her existence in creation and in the construction of new forms. Apollonian values increase the chances that culture and civilization will survive.

- Socratic values – according to them learning about and understanding oneself as well as perfecting one's personality are the highest good for a human being. Constant development, self-education and self-improvement are the greatest source of satisfaction for an individual. Life has a meaning inasmuch as it allows one to form a comprehensively developed personality. There is no gap between Apollonian and Socratic hierarchies. As for the former, what is the most important is the question of "how to get to know and change the outside world", while for the latter it is "how to get to know and design oneself" [Kozielecki 2000, p. 203-205; own translation].

It should be added that in real life it is rare for a human being to only fit into one of the above-mentioned categories. Usually, a human being is a kind of combination of these categories.

In the context of the introduced model of *Homo hedonismus*, it seems advisable to put forward the hypothesis that each of the above-mentioned categories denotes a hedonistic human being, but people belonging to different categories have adopted different definitions of pleasure and unpleasantness in the process of socialization.

Based on the overview of the above psychological conceptions of a human being and by having pointed to such of their elements that are consistent with AMHHB, one may formulate the hypothesis that all of the theories which are part of these conceptions and are not incompatible with the others are consistent with the proposed model of a hedonistic human being, which confirms that the adopted model is correct.

The subsequent chapters of this book deal with the influence that the socialization process has on human nature and the resulting possible changes in behavior – consumer behavior in particular.

CHAPTER FOUR
*
The socialization process and consumer decisions

Religion and culture play an important role in how patterns of behavior develop as well as in what decisions and choices we all make. Various patterns and habits are formed in the process of socialization. According to the adopted axiomatics of the concept of a hedonistic human being, people's behavior changes under the influence of the environment in which they grow up. This is also when new, subjective definitions of pleasure and unpleasantness are created and when habits are developed.

The influence of religion on consumer behavior (4.1)

Religion is a part of culture, but religion itself has such a huge impact on human behavior that I decided to separately discuss this topic in relation to the socialization process. Based on the multimedia *PWN* encyclopedia, the text below presents the most important facts about the largest religions in the world as well as their philosophical aspects. Among the most widespread religions are:

- Judaism – about 12-14 million followers,
- Christianity – about 1.85-2.1 billion followers,
- Islam – about 1.0-1.3 billion followers,
- Buddhism – about 500 million followers,
- Confucianism – about 160 million followers,
- Hinduism – about 900 million followers.

One of the most important messages of all these religions is that life continues after death. Each religion tempts its adherents with a kind of reward that they will receive if they behave properly during their lives. Most of all, they should follow the general principles of a given faith. The end of one's existence as well as death have always caused fear in people, and this fact is reflected in all religions. However, religions differ slightly when it comes to what awaits us after death. In simplified terms, it looks as follows:

- In Christianity, Islam, and Judaism, people are, after they die, judged for their deeds and faith during their lives. If the judgment is favorable, an individual obtains salvation, which ensures that he or she will live happily in heaven. However, depending on the religion, if the judgment is unfavorable, an individual's soul will die or will be sentenced to damnation, e.g. to life in hell which will be full of suffering, or to eternal separation from God.
- In Hinduism and Buddhism, reincarnation occurs after death – all creatures are born again and either enter a higher or lower level of existence, depending on their deeds during life.
- As for Confucianism, the worthy dead become a part of heaven, i.e. an impersonal entity guiding the world.

In each of the above-mentioned religions a human being must deserve to be given a reward in the form of an afterlife. Appropriate behavior during life is, most of all, characterized by ethical conduct in accordance with what God has ordained.

According to the second of the adopted axioms of a hedonistic human being's nature, people have an aversion to the risk of experiencing unpleasant things. This has been confirmed by Tversky and Kahneman's prospect theory. On the basis of this axiom it can be concluded that human religiousness is based on inborn risk aversion. Each of the major religions promises life after death, eternal life or another life in a new form, but the fulfillment of this promise is conditional upon proper behavior and the observance of a given religion's principles. Therefore, there is the age-old human fear of nothingness after death and a promise of further life if one behaves according to religious rules. Thus there is a great risk of not being given eternal (the next) life. This risk increases with age for every human being, which is reflected in the age structure of those who practice religion the most intensely. As people get older they inevitably approach the end of their lives and thus also the moment when they find out whether religious promises are true. It is thus not a coincidence that those for whom this risk is the highest, i.e. those who are the oldest in a given society, constitute the largest group among the most religious people. Behaviorists explain human religiousness in a very similar way – they believe that religious institutions operate by means of both positive and negative reinforcement. Eternal happiness after death is an example of the former, whereas eternal damnation is an example of the latter.

The above assumptions should never be regarded as criticism of any religion. I do not feel entitled to point to some religion as untrue or to state that one religion is better than another. The discussion presented above only points to the fact that people turn to religion because of their hedonistic nature.

Moreover, the religion that prevails in a given society undoubtedly has an influence on consumers' choices, e.g. the followers of Judaism must eat kosher food products, whereas the followers of Islam must not drink alcohol.

Also, the culture of a given social group plays an important role in shaping human behavior, decision-making processes and consumer choice. Such an attitude is consistent with the sixth of the proposed axioms of the theory of a hedonistic human being:

VI. *Homo hedonismus*'s unconscious is always oriented toward achieving pleasure, or a benefit, while his or her consciousness is shaped throughout his/her lifespan by the environment, i.e. by culture, religion, moral and legal principles, upbringing as well as

science, and this is why *Homo hedonismus* may take on attitudes other than hedonism.

The influence that religion has on social behaviors and a given society's culture is shown in a comparative table (Table 4.1.1) which has been prepared by K. Kietliński. It presents the way in which particular important issues that are related to human economic and consumer activity are seen from the perspective of the four major religions of the world.

Table 4.1.1. Positions taken by great religions on issues related to economic activity.

ISSUE	JUDAISM	BUDDHISM	CHRISTIANITY	ISLAM
WORK	It is a continuation of the work of Creation and is about transforming the world through work; industriousness is a guarantee of success and success at work is a sign of God's blessing and the act of building God's Kingdom.	It results from Buddha's eight proper attitudes; in Mahayana work is a way of freeing oneself from selfishness, i.e. it is a path to nirvana; perseverance is recommended while doing any kind of work so that a given product can be perfect; work is to help in achieving the common well-being of	It is a continuation of Creation; the capitalist work ethic was developed in Protestantism; according to this religion work is a secular service to God, while in Catholicism the significance of human work to the so-called Catholic social teaching is emphasized – it is to contribute to the comprehensive development of	Each activity is a service to Allah unless it is prohibited by the shariah; according to the Koran work is not punishment for a sin, but it does help a human being retain his or her dignity; an individual should strive to gain a high position by working; the Koran also recommends that people keep a balance between

THE MODEL OF A HEDONISTIC HUMAN BEING VERSUS THE SOCIAL RESPONSIBILITY OF CONSUMERS

			humankind.	humankind.	work and relaxation.
IDLENESS		It is a sin.	It is not a sin as it helps an individual free him- or herself from unnecessary wants.	It is a sin.	It is a sin.
A NON-WORKING DAY		It has a religious significance – people must celebrate the Sabbath (Saturday) which is a good thing because it was established by Yahweh on the seventh day of Creation.	No day off has been established; a non-working day is unsuitable because it gives people the opportunity to look for entertainment, which brings suffering.	Sunday must be celebrated to honor the memory of Christ's Resurrection; a non-working day is a good thing as it was given by God on the seventh day of Creation.	Formerly no day off was established; people stopped working in order to perform the noon prayer (on Friday); currently schools and stores are closed on Fridays; a day off is unsuitable because it usually results in neglect of the work of God.
VALUES		Justice, honesty, solidarity, compassion	Honesty, respect, kindness, loyalty, compassion, service to society, friendship	Love of one's neighbor, justice, moderation, common good, solidarity, helping others, subsidiarity	Honesty, kindness, justice, brotherhood, compassion
		It is respected; goods should	One should free him- or	The right to property is one	Nine out of ten of all goods

PRIVATE PROPERTY	serve the needs of all people; it is forbidden to waste or destroy goods.	herself from property which brings suffering; it is forbidden to waste resources.	of a human being's natural rights; people are stewards of material goods, not their owners; wastefulness is prohibited.	have been given by Allah; it is righteous to possess property; trade is the basis of the concept of property; wastefulness or the overuse of resources is prohibited.
ATTITUDE TO WEALTH	Favorable – possession of wealth is a sign of God's blessing.	One should free him- or herself from wealth because the desire for wealth brings suffering.	Favorable; at the same time one is warned against being tempted by greed.	Favorable
USURY	Prohibited; according to the law it can only be practiced with regard to strangers.	Prohibited	Prohibited	Prohibited
THE CONCEPT OF THE HUMAN BEING	A human being was created in the image of God.	A human being does not have a self, or a soul, because he or she is reborn in successive incarnations.	Human beings were created in the image of God, which is why they have a special kind of dignity.	The human being was created as Allah's deputy and should completely submit to God.
	Trade should be subject to the principles of Judaism; unfair competition is	It is not so much the profits as the service to society that counts; trade	In the beginning of Christianity trade was regarded as reprehensible because it was	Trade is to be conducted in accordance with Allah's will – "God willing", goods

TRADE	prohibited; openness; debts should be paid on time; one should adhere to the conditions of contracts; one should sell products of good quality; it is forbidden to falsify weights and measures or to sell products that are harmful to the user; one must not offer bribes.	should be based on the principle of justice; it is recommended that people buy and sell things that are necessary to life; it is forbidden to trade stimulants or arms materials that are destructive to people.	associated with greed; later, it gained acceptance mainly due to Protestantism; in Catholicism it is emphasized that trade should be based on respecting human dignity and on the principle of social solidarity; Christianity also contributed to the development of ethics in economics.	should only be gained in an honest way; it is recommended that trade be based on work (halal), whereas making profit on usury, gambling or doing harm to others is unacceptable (haram); trade is to contribute to the development of individuals and society.
HELPING THE POOR	Old Testament law required that people help the poor; it was believed that one who did not share with the needy stole from them, i.e. was a thief (banks for the poor).	It is recommended that people help the poor in order to overcome their own selfishness and develop an altruistic attitude.	It is recommended that people share with the poor and needy as this is a condition for salvation (caritas).	Giving alms is required by law – zakat (one-fortieth of one's property); one can deserve salvation by distributing one's goods to the poor.
THE PRINCIPLE OF JUSTICE	This principle results from the law; it is the basis of all economic	The principle is related to the fourth and fifth point of the so-called right	Justice is emphasized in Christian social teachings as a condition for	The importance of justice is emphasized in the Koran; one

	activity; according to this rule people had to pay taxes for the benefit of society and they also had to help the poor.	attitudes ("right action" and "right livelihood").	maintaining peace in the world.	should always avoid doing harm.
GREED	It was condemned in the Old Testament; it is regarded as a source of other wrongs such as jealousy, exploitation, lying, violence, or theft.	According to Buddha's teachings, greed is an evil desire which brings about suffering.	Greed is condemned in the New Testament; according to Catholic social teachings consumerism is a manifestation of greed.	Greed is condemned in the Koran because it leads people away from God, prayer and the practice of Islam.
POVERTY	It is undesirable; according to the Old Testament the poor themselves were to blame for their poverty, which was a result of laziness or neglect and, as such, was considered to be God's punishment	Poverty is recommended as a way of freeing oneself from desires which bring suffering; it brings one closer to nirvana.	It was recommended in early Christianity; in the Christian religion neither poverty nor wealth is in itself good or bad, but it is emphasized that one ought not to become attached to material objects, which should serve the needs of the whole society.	Poverty is not required; just as in Christianity, poverty itself does not ensure salvation; it is rather connected with a proper attitude toward material goods; it is recommended that people distribute their property to their relatives

	for one's sins.			and orphans.
ENTREPRENEURS HIP AND PROFIT	Entrepreneurship is recommended; according to the Talmud, Jehovah likes enterprising people better than pious ones; maximizing profits is not the only goal of companies and it is subject to certain limitations.	Entrepreneurship is recommended; a company is to make a profit, but first of all it should serve the needs of society.	Entrepreneurship is recommended; a company is to make a profit, but it should also take human and moral factors into account.	Entrepreneurship is recommended; companies are to serve the needs of individuals and society through the revenue they generate; the Koran mandated that employers ensure social security to their employees.
THE EMPLOYER AND REMUNERATION	According to the law of the Old Testament an employer is obligated to pay remuneration on time and to abide by the principle of justice.	An employer is to show respect and kindness to all the people employed at his or her company and to work together with them in the spirit of true charity.	According to the New Testament and the tradition of the Church, an employer is obligated to pay remuneration on time; Catholic social teaching adds that fair pay is such that it allows one to support his or her family.	An employer is obligated to pay proper remuneration to his or her employees, which is emphasized in the Koran; exploitation of workers is prohibited.
	On the basis of Old Testament law, one should show good	It is recommended that people overcome their selfishness and	People should treat others as ends in themselves, not instrumentally.	Social relations are regulated according to the shariah, which

SOCIAL RELATIONS	faith toward others.	become altruistic.		emphasizes that people should cooperate for the common good; the aim of giving alms is to restore social justice.
UNEMPLOYMENT	Unemployment should be tackled; different kinds of help to the unemployed are recommended, e.g. loans, training and retraining.	It is regarded as reprehensible because it means that society does not care about individual human beings.	It makes it more difficult to engage in one's calling both in earthly and eternal terms.	Efforts should be made to combat unemployment; it is the state's duty to guarantee employment to its citizens.
ECONOMY	It is emphasized that the stability of society depends on proper economic management; willful misconduct in business is a sign of lack of faith in Jehovah.	It is the people who are more important in production, not machines; technology should be subordinated to the human being; it is inappropriate to manufacture luxury products; one should save and seek a balance between production and consumption.	Christianity has developed the concept of social market economy; the capitalist economic system is accepted provided that it is committed to the common good; attention is drawn to the need for moderation in using resources and for complying with ecological requirements.	As regards economic management, a Muslim is responsible to Allah; it is forbidden to employ children or give women work that is too heavy; competition is recommended; in Islam financial contracts are signed in the form of financial

					agreements made by parties forming a business (shirkah) and in the form of an agency agreement (mudaraba).
THE GOLDEN RULE	"Do unto others as you would have them do unto you"	"Hurt not others in ways that you yourself would find hurtful"		"So whatever you wish that others would do to you, do also to them"	"Not one of you is a believer until he loves for his brother what he loves for himself"

Source: [Kietliński 2006: 52-56, own translation]

The above table shows how great an influence the great monotheistic religions have on the rules of economic management and consumption. People who were raised in one of the above-mentioned religious environments will behave in a way that is, to a certain extent, consistent with the rules of that given religion. This is very important both when it comes to consumer decisions and to the strategies adopted by the businesses that operate in those cultural areas. As for the concept of *Homo hedonismus* that has been introduced, this means that a human being's consciousness may take on attitudes other than the hedonistic ones according to the sixth axiom. However, it should also be noted that such an image of the human being will usually be subjective and external – people adopt social attitudes that are compatible with a given religion due to their hedonistic nature and loss aversion (e.g. the loss of eternal life).

The influence of culture on consumer behavior (4.2)

The culture of a given society in which a given person is born and lives has an important impact on many aspects of his or her consumption-related decisions. The Dutch sociologist Geert Hofstede is one of the well-known researchers on organizational culture who carried out extensive research studies in this area in the 1960s and the 1970s. He conducted a survey of IBM employees and identified the types of organizational culture; then he described national cultures based on the results of these analyses.

Geert Hofstede defines culture as collective programming of the human mind which distinguishes members of a given group or category from other groups or categories of people [Hofstede 2007, p. 17]. Every human being's mind is programmed. This programming is partially the same for all people and partially typical of and specific to one person only. Hofstede identified three levels of mental programming (Figure 4.2.2):

- universal,
- characteristic of a given group or category,
- individual.

According to Hofstede, human nature represents the universal level which is common to all human beings and which is genetically inherited and related to knowledge concerning basic physical and psychological needs. Culture pertains to the collective level which is characteristic of a given social group and is acquired in the process of socialization from previous generations. Personality represents a level that is unique and specific to a given individual.

National identity is a factor that most differentiates people from one another. It is a reflection of the cultural programming of their minds and it shapes their values, norms, attitudes, perception of the world, and behavior, including consumer behavior.

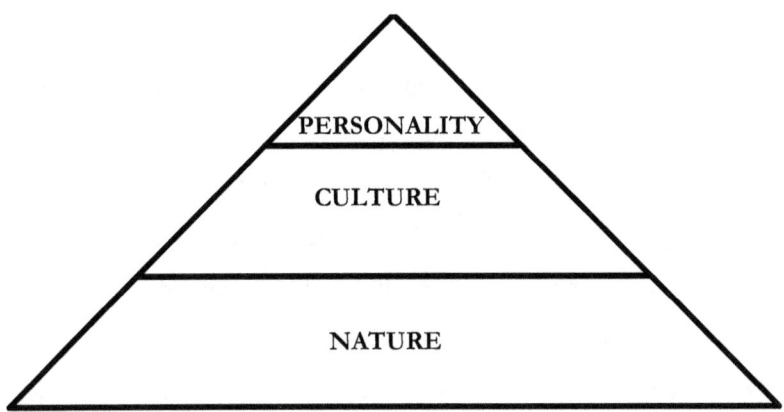

Figure 4.2.2. Levels of mental programming.

Source: Hofstede, Hofstede 2007: 18

The dimensions of each culture were established as a result of Hofstede's research [Hofstede 1980, 2001]. At the beginning four such dimensions were identified and then in 1991 and 2010[2] two more were added. These dimensions describe every culture in the world and at the same time point to the differences between cultures.

In order to demonstrate what influence different cultures might have on consumer behavior, a short description of particular cultural dimensions is presented below:

---

[2] Usually five dimensions are mentioned in the literature; for information about the sixth dimension see *The Hofstede Centre*'s website at: www.geert-hofstede.com. This website also presents the results of measurements of particular cultural dimensions for many countries of the world.

- Power distance index (PDI) – defines the relations between superiors and subordinates as well as between the government and its citizens; it also refers to the extent to which social inequalities are accepted.
- Collectivism vs individualism (IDV) – describes the proportion of the importance of the individual to the importance of groups and identifies the roles that are assigned to individuals and groups.
- Femininity vs masculinity (MAS) – describes the differentiation of roles adopted by the sexes and the rigidity of these roles. In a masculine society there is a significant division of roles between the sexes, whereas in a feminine society such a division is not as sharp.
- Uncertainty avoidance index (UAI) – specifies the extent to which the members of a given culture feel insecure in the face of new, unknown or uncertain situations.
- Long-term vs short-term orientation (LTO) – refers to the differentiation between a long- and short-term perspective on life. Long-term orientation focuses on the future, whereas short-term orientation on the present and on the past.
- Indulgence vs restraint (IVR) – describes the difference between a tendency to satisfy one's needs easily and the rigid norms that regulate and curb one's enjoyment of life.

The summary below, which presents the most important elements of cultural dimensions that have a direct or indirect influence on consumption, shows how particular dimensions of culture impact consumer behavior and the principles of decision-making (Table 4.2.3).

Table 4.2.3. Elements of Geert Hofstede's cultural dimensions that have a direct or indirect influence on consumer behavior.

CULTURAL DIMENSION	FIRST ELEMENT OF THIS DIMENSION	SECOND ELEMENT OF THIS DIMENSION
LOW VS HIGH POWER DISTANCE	Parents treat children as equals. Children should play. Children are no guarantee of security to their elderly parents. Small businesses are set up for professional reasons. Flat organizational pyramids Subordinates are consulted. Little difference between the salaries of employees at the top and the bottom of the organizational ladder Physical work has the same status as office work. Power, status, and income do not have to go together. Small income differences in society; these differences are further reduced through the tax system. A low corruption rate; scandals end political careers. Citizens read newspapers. Privileges and signs of status	Parents require obedience from their children. Children should work hard. Children guarantee security to their elderly parents. Small businesses are set up in order to run a family business. Steep organizational pyramids Subordinates are told what to do. A large difference between the salaries of employees at the top and the bottom of the organizational ladder Office work is valued more than physical work. Status factors co-occur: power entails status and wealth. Large income differences in society; the differences are further exacerbated by the tax system. A high corruption rate: scandals are covered up. Citizens watch television.

	are not approved of. Exercising authority should be sanctioned by law and be based on the criteria of good and evil. Everyone should have equal rights. The privilege of authority is determined by the post that one officially holds as well as by one's competence and ability to reward others	Privileges and signs of status are commonly recognized and accepted. Power is above the law: a position of authority grants one the privilege of infallibility and is identified with doing good. People in power should have privileges. The privilege of authority is determined by connections, charisma and the ability to reward others.
COLLECTIVISM VS INDIVIDUALISM	People belong to multigenerational families or other groups which give them protection and security in return for loyalty. One must not oppose one's parents. People share their earnings with family members and maintain their family. It is obvious that one must take part in family celebrations (it is the participation that counts, it does not matter if one sits in silence or not). Individual initiatives are stifled. Diplomas provide access to higher-status groups. The relations between an employer and an employee are seen in moral terms and they resemble family ties. Decisions concerning	Everyone lives to take care of oneself and one's immediate family. Children earn their living themselves (e.g. they earn money for college). Family meetings are rather awkward and make people feel compelled to communicate verbally. Self-reliance is encouraged. Diplomas increase one's economic status and self-esteem. Assertiveness The relationship between an employer and an employee is a contract that brings mutual benefits. Decisions concerning employment and promotion are based on the regulations in force and depend on

COLLECTIVISM VS INDIVIDUALISM	employment and promotion are based on employees' group membership.

Interpersonal relationships are more important than achieving goals.

Sons follow in their fathers' footsteps when it comes to choosing an occupation.

One employs his or her family members.

The interest of the group is more important than the interest of the individual.

Private life is dominated by the group.

Opinions held by an individual depend on the group he or she belongs to.

The gross national product per capita is low.

The state plays a dominant role in the economy.

The press is controlled by the government.

People are encouraged to show sadness; a display of joy in not acceptable.

Consumption patterns indicate that people are dependent on others.

Personal contacts and ties are the main source of information.

People with disabilities bring shame on their families and | employees' abilities and achievements.

Achieving a goal is more important that interpersonal relationships.

Sons' occupations are different from their fathers'.

Employing family members is very undesirable.

The interest of the individual is more important than the interest of the group.

Everyone has the right to a private life.

Everyone should have their own opinion.

The gross national product per capita is high.

The state has a limited role in the economy.

Freedom of the press

People are encouraged to show joy; a display of sadness in not accepted.

Consumption patterns indicate that people are independent and self-reliant.

The mass media are the main source of information.

People with disabilities should participate in normal life as much as possible.

Task achievement is more |

	should be isolated. Interpersonal relationships are more important than task achievement. The Internet and electronic mail do not seem attractive and are rarely used.	important than interpersonal relationships. The Internet and electronic mail are seen as a very attractive means of communication and are often used for contacting others.
FEMININITY VS. MASCULINITY	Failures in school are accepted as life's difficulties. The possibility of self-fulfillment and personal interests are decisive when choosing a job. Social alienation is a cause of suicides. One works to live. Managers are guided by intuition and they seek to reach agreement. What is important is equality, solidarity and the quality of one's work life. The dominant religion emphasizes gender equality. The emancipation of women at home and at work means equal rights and duties for both sexes. It is the woman who decides on the number of children the couple will have. There is a balance between work and family life. Relationships with other people and the quality of life are important. Parents usually share	Failures in school are a life tragedy. The prospect of a brilliant career is the main deciding factor in choosing employment for students. Poor performance in school is a cause of suicides. One lives to work. Managers should make decisive decisions and be assertive. What is important is justice, competition at work and achievement. The dominant religion emphasizes the superiority of the male sex. The emancipation of women means that they are admitted to positions that are usually occupied by men only. It is the man who decides on the size of the family. Work is more important than family. It is the challenges, earnings and progress that are important. The standard situation is that

		responsibilities connected with earning a living and care.	the father works and the mother takes care of the house.
		Sex is a way of establishing contact between people.	It is forbidden to openly discuss sex, but there is much veiled erotic symbolism.
		Sexual harassment is not a serious problem.	Sexual harassment is a serious problem.
		Homosexuality is treated as part of the natural order of things.	Homosexuality poses a threat to society.
		Both men and women buy food and cars.	Women buy food, whereas men buy cars.
		Couples share a car.	Couples have two cars.
		People buy more products for use at home.	People buy more products that increase their status.
		The Internet is used for building relationships with people.	The Internet is used for collecting data and information.
		People are paid according to the principle of equality.	People are paid according to the principle of equity.
		One's free time is more valuable than additional remuneration.	Additional remuneration is more valuable than free time.
		Both sexes can freely choose to pursue a career.	It is the men's duty to make a career, whereas women are free to choose if they want to pursue a career
		Greater participation of women in the professional labor market.	Lower participation of women in the professional labor market
		A welfare society is the ideal society (common well-being); the needy deserve support.	An efficient society is the ideal society; the best deserve support.
		People attach much importance to the protection of the natural environment; small is beautiful.	People attach much importance to constant economic growth; big is

	Religions with lenient rules. The attitude of religion to the pleasure of sex is positive or neutral.	beautiful. Religions with stringent rules Religion treats sex as a means of procreation and not as recreation.
LOW VS HIGH UNCERTAINTY AVOIDANCE	Uncertainty is a natural part of life; one should accept life as it is. Low levels of stress; a subjective sense of well-being People do not show aggression or feelings openly. Ambiguous and risky situations do not cause fear. Children are given very general guidelines about what is unclean or forbidden. Different means interesting. Time is a guide. People have a positive attitude to idleness – one does not necessarily have to work hard. It requires special effort to be precise and punctual. Different, innovative activities and ideas are accepted. Achievement and recognition are the main motivators. There are few general laws and	Uncertainty that is typical of life is a constant threat which must be counteracted. High levels of stress; a subjective feeling of anxiety It is allowed to give vent to aggression and one's feelings at the right time and place. People accept risk which has been tamed; they fear ambiguous situations and the risk of the unknown. There are strict rules that tell children precisely what is unclean and forbidden. Different means dangerous. Time is money. People have a strong need to be constantly occupied and an inner need for hard work. People have a natural tendency to be precise and punctual. People have a strong emotional need to codify everything into laws and regulations even if such laws and regulations do not work in practice. People who behave differently and have different views are persecuted; there is a

	rules.	reluctance to introduce innovations.
	If regulations or rules are not complied with, they should be changed.	Security, recognition or a sense of belonging are the main motivators.
	Civil protests are socially accepted.	There are many detailed rules and laws.
	Citizens are very competent when it comes to the authorities.	Citizens are incompetent when it comes to the authorities.
	Citizens have a positive attitude toward the state's institutions.	If people do not comply with rules, they are sinners and should repent for their sins.
	Civil servants have a positive attitude to politics.	Civil protests should be suppressed.
	Tolerance and moderation	Citizens have a negative attitude toward the state's institutions.
	The attitude toward young people is friendly.	Civil servants have a negative attitude to politics.
	Regionalism and internationalism, attempts to integrate minorities into society.	Conservatism, extremism, law and order
	Opinions held by one group should not be imposed on others.	The attitude toward young people is hostile.
	Human rights: no one should be persecuted on the grounds of his or her beliefs.	Nationalism and xenophobia, minorities are persecuted.
	Changing jobs is not a problem.	People have faith in specialists and experts.
	People take ethical considerations into account more often when doing the shopping.	There is only one truth and we know it.
		There is religious, political and ideological fundamentalism as well as intolerance.
	Family life goes on peacefully.	Family life is full of stress and tension.
	People have fewer concerns	

	about their health and money. There are many nurses and few doctors. The goods that people buy are to provide comfort. New products and technologies, such as the Internet, e-mail and cell phones, are quickly accepted. People make risky investment decisions. Advertisements employ a sense of humor. The focus is on the decision-making process. Liberalism	People have more concerns about their health and money. There are many doctors and few nurses. The goods that people buy have to meet the requirements of being clean and tidy. People are indecisive and afraid of new products and technologies. People make conservative investment decisions. Advertisements make use of expert knowledge. The focus is on the content of the decisions one makes. Conservatism, law and order
SHORT-TERM ORIENTATION VS LONG-TERM ORIENTATION	Respect for tradition People respect social and statutory obligations regardless of the incurred cost. There is social pressure to "keep up with the Joneses" even if this entails excessive spending. A low saving rate, limited investment funds People expect quick results. People care about "saving their face".	Traditions are adapted to modern conditions. People respect social and statutory obligations to a limited extent. People are thrifty and use resources in a cost-effective way. A high saving rate, large investment funds People patiently wait for long-term results. People are willing to comply with the objectives.

THE MODEL OF A HEDONISTIC HUMAN BEING VERSUS THE SOCIAL RESPONSIBILITY OF CONSUMERS

	The quest for the truth	People aim to adhere to the principles of righteousness.
	There are universal guidelines about what is good and what is bad.	What is right and what is wrong depends on the circumstances.
	Marriage is a moral obligation.	Marriage is a pragmatic arrangement.
	Old age begins late, but it is a period of life that is devoid of joy.	Old age begins quite early, but it is a happy period of life.
	Among the main values associated with work are: freedom, an individual's rights, achievement, and thinking about oneself.	Among the main values associated with work are: the possibility of learning, honesty, the ability to adapt, and self-discipline.
	There exist universal rules for determining what is good and what is evil.	What is right and what is wrong depends on the circumstances.
		Large social and economic differences are not accepted.
	A condescending attitude toward others	Humility
	People invest in trust funds.	People invest in real property.
	People believe in folk wisdom and witchcraft.	People have faith in knowledge and education.
INDULGENT SOCIETIES VS RESTRAINING SOCIETIES	There is a high percentage of people who state that they are happy.	There are few happy people.
	People have control over their own lives.	People feel helpless.
		Freedom of speech is not that important.
	Freedom of speech is important.	Pleasures are not a priority.
	Pleasures are important.	In educated societies there is a low population growth rate.
	In educated societies there is a high population growth rate.	Few people do sports.
		In wealthy societies there is a

	Many people do sports.	small percentage of obese people.
	In wealthy societies there is a large percentage of obese people.	In wealthy countries there are strict sexual standards.
	In wealthy countries there are loose sexual standards.	There is a large number of police officers in relation to the population.
	Maintaining social order is not a high priority.	Cynicism
	Leisure time is of higher importance.	Leisure time is of lower importance.
	Friends are important.	Friends are not that important.
	People attach little importance to thrift and savings.	People attach much importance to thrift and savings.
	People have a greater tendency to remember positive emotions.	People have a lesser tendency to remember positive emotions.
	People are more optimistic.	People are more pessimistic.
	People are more satisfied with their family life.	People are less satisfied with their family life.
	People eat less fish.	People eat more fish.
	People drink more beverages and beer.	People drink less beverages and beer.
	A smile is the norm.	A smile raises suspicion.

Source: own work based on Hofstede 2011, and Hofstede, Hofstede and Minkov 2010.

The above table shows how different the world's cultures can be. All of the elements of the cultural dimensions that have been presented here can also occur in intermediate states: there is a great variety of possible cultures and different combinations of these cultures have a different influence on the principles of consumption. One can see how different and how extreme consumers' attitudes can be when analyzing each of the components of these cultural dimensions. When looking at particular components one can notice that some of them are purely hedonistic in character, like human nature. Some examples of these are:

- Everyone lives to take care of oneself and one's immediate family
- The relationship between an employer and an employee is a contract that brings mutual benefits
- The interest of the individual is more important than the interest of the group
- One works to live
- Sex is a way of establishing contact between people
- People have a positive attitude toward idleness – one does not necessarily have to work hard
- If regulations or rules are not complied with, they should be changed
- The goods that people buy are to provide comfort
- Pleasures are important

When combining Hofstede's concept with the idea of a hedonistic human being one can put forward the hypothesis that human nature is reflected in the very axiomatics of the *Homo hedonismus* theory, that culture is a result of one's geographical location and position within a social group, and that one's personality is a combination of human nature and all of the results of the influence that a given environment exerts on this nature. Such an environment is understood as being made up of religion, norms and values, as well as of one's family and the social group one belongs to. One's personality, in turn, is manifested as the consciousness, whereas one's nature is hidden in the unconscious.

The broad range of possible human behaviors shows how deeply the socialization process can influence human nature. However, this does not mean that people cease to be hedonistic; it only shows how profoundly culture can distort human nature and how strong the aversion to the risk of experiencing unpleasantness must be in some societies (i.e. unpleasantness resulting from breaching a given culture's rules) if people are willing to adapt to such unnatural principles of conduct. The existence of social movements demanding changes shows that many of the rules that have been presented in the table are unnatural.

When summarizing the discussion of psychological conceptions of humankind it is also worthwhile to take a look at an important principle governing human behavior. Cialdini [2007] points to many such rules, but it is one of them in particular that is of special significance and further shows what real human nature is like. It is called 'reciprocity' and is one of the most common principles of conduct in all cultures. This principle is about creating a sense of obligation to reciprocate, in a similar way, the good (benefit) one has received. This means that the one who gives something to someone obtains a "guarantee" that such an act will not entail an irretrievable loss. In practice this rule shows that, in the course of social development, a mechanism has emerged which has its roots in hedonism and which is incredibly important for the creation of different chains of exchanges as well as transactions and relationships. The following research example illustrates how hedonistic this principle is:

Guests who have been invited to a wedding reception find out that the couple expects to be given cash only. They can, however, hand over this gift in two alternative ways: in an envelope together with the wedding congratulations cards or in an anonymous envelope which is to be put into a special basket.

A survey was conducted in which the guests were asked whether they would put the same amount of money in both kinds of envelopes. It turns out that a majority of the respondents said they would put a smaller sum in an anonymous envelope than in an envelope containing a congratulations card. This example shows that if we are "sure" that we can expect reciprocity then we will give a larger amount of money because we hope to be given a similar sum in return in the future.

Sensory deprivation vs consumer choices (4.3)

In order to establish what influence the environment has on consumer decisions a research study was carried out with the aim of determining the way in which people make decisions under conditions of sensory deprivation. Total sensory deprivation means that one receives no information coming from the outside and that, in practice, a human being is devoid of senses. In such a situation there is no selection process because a lack of information would mean a lack of alternatives. At the same time it should be noted that the sense of sight is the most important of the senses that provide information about the external world to people. Therefore, deprivation of sight provides an interesting research case which may help in establishing how such circumstances influence consumers' decisions and social behaviors. This situation is a special example of information asymmetry as, in such an extreme state, a consumer has almost no access to information.

A healthy human being has five senses, namely sight, hearing, smell, taste and touch. All people use each of the senses to a certain extent while making consumer choices and all of the senses have some impact on one's final decision. The research study involved interviewing and observing people who had lost their sense of sight. The text below presents several basic rules that such people are governed by when making consumer choices.

- Advertisements do not encourage people to buy a given product and they can even lead to a negative evaluation of a product when they are too intrusive or inappropriately worded.
- Packaging does not influence consumers' decisions whatsoever.
- As for food products, people are inclined to choose unprocessed products which have been manufactured in reliable facilities (eggs from small rural farms, organically grown vegetables) and they draw up lists of trusted products.
- The choice of clothing is made based on whether particular clothes are comfortable and made from quality materials as well as based on the quality of workmanship (which is assessed by using the sense of touch). Such a choice is also determined by the practicality of a given product and by the possible color preferences of people who have become blind, but it is not determined by a product's appearance, other people's impressions of the product or the product's brand.
- People choose where to do their shopping based on their previous experience with the quality of service. Personal contact with a salesperson is very important.
- People usually do not trust information about products that is provided by those products' producers.
- Consumers ask for the opinions of other people whom they trust based on their previous positive experiences with such opinions.
- Any goods that act as substitutes for the sense one has lost are a priority for consumers as they help them reduce the fear of becoming dependent on others and help them gain as much independence as possible. These are, for example, devices that verbally inform people

about the state of a particular thing or provide some other information, e.g. a talking thermometer, watch, telephone, or computer.

- As for one's aspirations and personal motivation, it is a priority to have as much interpersonal contact with others as possible, which can also somehow substitute for the loss of a given sense. The people in one's surroundings become those who provide information about the outside world. Moreover, the need for recognition and self-actuation is very important, in particular with regard to those areas in which the lack of a given sense is not an obstacle.

When analyzing the results of the above-mentioned study, one must state that a lack of one of the senses leads to a distortion (change) of the influence that socialization exerts on an individual, which is manifested, for example, in that a person who has lost one of his or her senses applies a different procedure to and hierarchy for evaluating products than people who use all of their senses. It should also be noted that a lack of one of the senses does not affect human nature which, one way or another, is still a *Homo hedonismus*'s nature. Such a situation, however, clearly has an impact on how people who have lost one of their senses define pleasures and threats (i.e. differently than others). The above experiment indicates that a given environment, which is understood as a set of information items that are supplied to an individual by all of his or her senses, is an important factor in consumer decision-making, which means that the environment influences human behavior. On the other hand, one can see that a lack of one of the senses leads to the development of specific autonomous procedures that are employed when making decisions without information that would be otherwise supplied by the missing sense.

CHAPTER FIVE

*

Verifying the model of a hedonistic human being by means of a research experiment

A research experiment was conducted in the years 2010-2012 in order to confirm that the proposed model of a human being is correct. Many people may intuitively disagree with the axiomatics that has been adopted for this model, and will say that arguing that human beings are subjective and non-rational creatures or that individualizing the definition of a benefit (pleasure) is pointless – but science has rules – and a theory will not constitute a scientific theory but will only be common or intuitive knowledge until it is scientifically verified or falsified. This experiment did not aim to confirm all of the adopted axioms of the model but only some of them, i.e. the following:

- *Homo hedonismus* seeks to achieve subjective pleasure, or a benefit, and to achieve its maximum amount, as subjectively perceived.
- *Homo hedonismus* has both a short-term and a long-term aversion to risk – it is a fear of the risk of not obtaining pleasure, or a benefit, or the fear of experiencing something unpleasant.
- Every *Homo hedonismus* might individually arrive at his or her own subjective definition of pleasure and a benefit, which may change during his or her lifetime due to the influence of his/her environment.
- *Homo hedonismus*'s unconscious is always oriented toward achieving pleasure, or a benefit, while his or her consciousness is shaped throughout his/her lifespan by the environment, i.e. by culture, religion, moral and legal principles, upbringing as well as science, and that is why *Homo hedonismus* may take on attitudes other than hedonism.

However, since it has already been shown that the model is compatible with many economic and psychological theories, it is assumed that if the hypotheses that have been put forward as part of this research study are verified, this will sufficiently prove that the whole model of *Homo hedonismus* is consistent with the real nature of consumer behavior.

At the same time, scientific objectivity requires that one point out that the exact economic and social situations of the study's participants are not known, which is a drawback because the purchase decisions they make might result from this very factor. On the other hand, what is known is that all of the participants have a comparable income, which is important because this should cause the whole studied group to make similar consumer choices. Another advantage of this experiment is that the participants are not aware that it is their purchase choices that will be analyzed and that the actual choices of products will be determined by taking into account the very act of the purchase and not, for example, by expressing the intention to buy a given product. These circumstances are an important feature of this study because they will make it possible to present the studied group's real consumer behaviors.

Description of the research method

The research experiment was based on comparing consumer choices that were made during a pre-holiday period (Christmas) by a group of participants (approx. 150 people). The group was homogeneous as regards income; the members of this group had the same amount of money at their disposal, i.e. PLN 300-350 (approx. USD 98-114). The fact that the studied group was homogeneous in terms of income was of vital importance because, theoretically, potential consumer choices should be similar. If income is distributed unevenly then one can expect *a priori* that people's preferences regarding the choice of products to buy will be varied. The participants in the experiment did not know that it was their consumer choices that would be analyzed, which was important because that made it possible to observe natural consumer behaviors. The participants were to make their purchases in one supermarket during a period of four weeks. They had to spend the whole sum of money (vouchers) in a single shopping session, and the unused part of the vouchers' value was lost. After all of the participants had made their purchases, a summary of the goods they had bought was prepared, on the basis of which their consumer behaviors were then analyzed for the purpose of verifying the proposed hypotheses.

Description of the research experiment

1. The selected sample group consisted of approx. 150 employees of one company who were at a similar income level. They earned approximately the national average, i.e. about gross PLN 3,600 (approx. USD 1,170) per month.
2. Three to four weeks before Christmas each member of the sample group received vouchers with identical values (PLN 300-350 [approx. USD 98-114]) which were to be exchanged in one supermarket for any goods it offered until Christmas time.
3. This experiment was repeated three times in the years: 2010, 2011 and 2012.
4. The receipts that all the members of the sample group received for all of the products they had bought as well as a summary report obtained from the supermarket constituted the research material.
5. The participants did not now that their purchasing decisions were being studied.

Research hypotheses

The following research hypotheses have been formulated according to the adopted model of a hedonistic human being. These hypotheses will either confirm that this model correctly reflects the nature of people's consumer behavior or they will falsify it.

H1: All of the receipts will vary as to the purchased products, i.e. there will be no two (or more) identical receipts (for the same products).

If this hypothesis is confirmed this will mean that every human being has different, subjective preferences and different, subjective priorities with respect to the products he or she buys. This will also prove that consumer choices are non-rational and that people do not pursue objective maximization of utility.

H2: A large portion of the purchased products will not have a utilitarian value connected with fulfilling one's physiological needs; they will be "pleasurable" products. This will be true for both food and non-food products. Repeatability of the products will be low.

If this hypothesis is confirmed this will mean that people seek to obtain pleasure. If repeatability of the purchased products will be low, this will additionally confirm that the definition of pleasure is subjective.

H3: The unused amount that is covered by the vouchers will be small and will constitute less than 1% of the vouchers' value.

If this hypothesis is confirmed than this will mean that the axiom that people have an aversion to the risk of experiencing unpleasantness will be verified. Here, unpleasantness will amount to wasting a larger part of one's voucher as a result of choosing wrong products in terms of their value.

Results of the research experiment

The basic values and indicators obtained from an analysis of the source material that was used for the purpose of the experiment are presented in Table 5.1.

Table 5.1. Summary of the research experiment's results

Year	2010	2011	2012
Number of participants in the research study	148	143	140
Value of the vouchers per one participant in PLN (USD)	350.00 (approx. 114.00)	350.00 (approx. 114.00)	300.00 (approx. 98.00)
Total value of the vouchers in PLN (USD)	51,800.00 (approx. 16,873.00)	50,050.00 (approx. 16,303.00)	42,000.00 (approx. 13,681.00)
Total value of the purchased products in PLN (USD)	51,541.62 (approx. 16,792.00)	49,834.87 (approx. 16,233.00)	41,733.91 (approx. 13,594.00)
Percentage (%) of the amount of money covered by the vouchers that was not spent	-0.4988%	-0.4298%	-0.6335%
Total number of different products (pieces) bought by the participants	4,801	3,993	3,528
Total number of products bought by the participants – pieces (sold by the piece)	8,553	7,042	6,241
Total weight of products bought by the participants – kilograms (sold by the kilogram)	840.17	676.53	474.50
Average number of different products bought by one participant	32.44	27.92	25.20

Average weight of all products bought by one participant (1 piece = 1 kg)	63.47	53.98	47.97
Total number of products bought as single pieces (% of the number of all different products)	2,749 (57.26%)	2,247 (56.27%)	2,060 (58.39%)
Percentage (%) of products bought at a standard VAT rate	50.82%	52.00%	51.57%
Percentage (%) of products bought at a reduced VAT rate	49.18%	48.00%	48.43%
Average value of one product in PLN and USD	5.49 (approx. 1.79)	6.46 (approx. 2.10)	6.21 (approx. 2.02)
Number of different products of which at least ten pieces were bought by the participants (% of the number of all different products bought by the participants)	69 (1.44%)	54 (1.35%)	58 (1.64%)
Number of different products of which at least ten kilograms were bought by the participants (% of the number of all different products bought by the participants)	11 (0.23%)	6 (0.15%)	4 (0.11%)

It should be noted that the average number of different products offered by the store that was covered by this experiment is 55,000-60,000. All products at this store are sold in two units of measure only, i.e. pieces and kilograms.

For the purpose of analyzing the source data the following assumptions were made in order to conduct the statistical calculations:

- In order to convert the units of measure it was assumed that 1 piece = 1 kilogram, but calculations concerning single items were only made for items whose quantity was expressed in pieces.
- Products that were referred to as purchased in larger quantities were those of which ten or more pieces, or ten or more kilograms, were bought.

The conclusions were derived from the analysis of data presented in the table above and from the source data.

1. In any of the years covered by this experiment no two identical sets of products were bought by different participants, which means that hypothesis H1 has been confirmed.
2. The value of the vouchers that was lost due to an imprecise selection of products in terms of their value (the sum of their prices) ranged from 0.4% to 0.6% of the overall value of the vouchers, which means that hypothesis H3 has been verified.
3. Statistically, each of the participants purchased 25-32 products that were not bought by any of the other participants. This means that the participants' preferences regarding the choice of products were varied and that there were very different subjective definitions of pleasure, which is consistent with the definition of sales as a subjectively non-equivalent exchange; this, in turn, verifies hypotheses H1 and H2.
4. Statistically speaking, in all of the years during which this experiment was being conducted, over 50% of each set of products consisted of products that were not part of any other product set, which additionally confirms hypotheses H1 and H2.
5. The fact that products which were taxed at the standard rate constituted more than half of all of the purchased goods and that this is the rate that applies to highly processed (food) products as well as to most non-food products means that the function of the majority of the purchased products was not to fulfill one's basic needs but to provide pleasure, which confirms hypothesis H2.
6. The products of which ten or more pieces, or ten or more kilograms, were bought comprised only somewhat less than 2% of all the

products, which means that repeatability of the purchased products was low, and it confirms hypothesis H2.

All of the results presented above and the conclusions derived from this research experiment are consistent with the proposed hypotheses, which further confirms that the axioms of a hedonistic human being which have been adopted here are correct.

CHAPTER SIX

*

The model of *Homo hedonismus* in management science

The importance of the model of a hedonistic human being in management science (6.1)

The new model of a human being that has been adopted here and has theoretically been confirmed by showing that it is consistent with other theories is of vital importance to the development of management science and related disciplines. Each of the established axioms is a kind of guideline for strategic marketing. All marketing tools can be appropriately adapted to this new model so that the organizational strategy can be planned and implemented even more effectively.

One can also ask the question as to whether this model is a completely new idea. From observing many of the marketing strategies adopted by different businesses it can be concluded that the answer is "no". Marketing products such as discount cards or cashback cards and advertisements referring to human sexuality testify to the fact that companies have intuitively known for a long time what human nature is like. The proposed model only systematizes this instinctive practical knowledge and introduces it to the world of science. As was shown in the introduction to this book, this model is also not a new idea in economics; it represents a return to conceptions which were created a long time ago and which might not have had a chance to be widely accepted at that time. In my opinion, these concepts were not accepted then because of people's reluctance to acknowledge that our nature is hedonistic and because the level of consumption was too low to make it possible to easily verify these theories in an empirical way.

Homo hedonismus is a model of a human being which above all allows one to descriptively present consumer behavior. In particular, it should be used to describe all phenomena related to consumer choices and decisions.

In this area, responsible consumption is one important issue which is inextricably bound with the concept of corporate social responsibility (CSR). Many businesses that have decided to implement the CSR concept need information about the level of consumer social responsibility (ConSR) in the markets where they operate as well as information on what might stimulate development of this responsibility.

Many international organizations and national governments are in favor of implementing the concept of sustainable development. Responsible behavior is to be a recipe for the climate change that is being observed and for the ever-growing problems arising from the scarcity of natural resources that economies now face.

This idea can only be put into practice when we achieve a high level of social responsibility in its three dimensions, i.e. corporate social responsibility, government social responsibility, and consumer social responsibility. The first two dimensions pertain to the responsibility of collective entities whose decision-making processes are often collective in character as well as influenced by many different stakeholders, which is why the adopted model of a human being does not directly apply to this sector. This model can only be used without any limitations with regard to the social responsibility of consumers; in this area the model constitutes the right tool for analyzing and predicting possible changes in consumer behavior. Therefore, the second part of this book will be devoted to the issue of ConSR, which will be discussed in the context of the model of a hedonistic human being. As far as management science is concerned, this part of the book has both a theoretical and applied character and may provide a basis for further theoretical reflection as well as practical guidelines on the strategic decisions that are made by businesses.

Three dimensions of social responsibility (6.2)

It is now time to clearly state that socially responsible actions cannot simply be a fad or just one of the possible organizational strategies but rather an absolute necessity with regard to the three different dimensions of social responsibility. Corporate social responsibility is currently the most common dimension of social responsibility. An increasing number of publications has also appeared on the topic of consumer social responsibility. Government social responsibility, however, is very rarely discussed. It looks as though only businesses and, possibly, consumers should be socially responsible but not necessarily governments. Does this mean that politicians only talk about sustainable development and social responsibility but they themselves do almost nothing? This is, unfortunately, to a large extent true.

All of the dimensions of social responsibility are interrelated (Fig. 6.2.1); CSR and ConSR depend on GSR, whereas CSR and ConSR are interdependent. The lack of an adequate, socially responsible state policy greatly hinders the emergence of both CSR and ConSR, and their development can be compromised without the state's support. Governmental support is particularly necessary in the initial phase of the development of CSR and ConSR. Such help mostly entails creating a legal system which would be consistent with the assumptions behind CSR and ConSR and which would particularly support the activities of businesses acting in accordance with CSR's principles and would positively influence consumer decisions in this regard. A properly adjusted fiscal law which would promote products that are manufactured according to the idea of CSR should be a tool for putting such ideas into action.

It should be noted that – as far as companies and governments are concerned – decisions are made by social groups (the management board or the political parties in power), thus the adopted model of a hedonistic human being cannot be directly implemented there. In addition, various stakeholders exert an influence on the decisions these groups make, which further complicates the decision-making process. Although each member of these groups is a *Homo hedonismus* by nature, collaborative work creates conflicts of interest and causes that a large number of different definitions of pleasure will clash, which in turn translates into more complex decision-making processes.

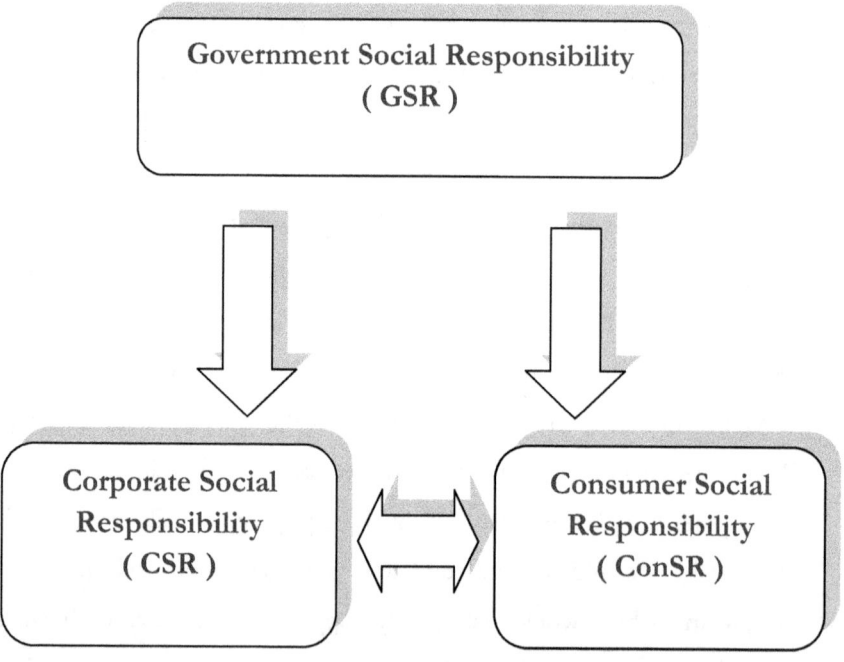

Fig.6.2.1. Interdependencies – interaction between the three dimensions of social responsibility.

Therefore, later in this book an attempt will be made to describe only the socially responsible behavior of consumers which results from individual decisions, whereas a description of the decision-making processes of social groups is beyond the scope of this book. I only want to draw attention to the complex issue of social responsibility which should be discussed with regard to its three dimensions. The other dimensions of social responsibility will only be presented in relation to the social responsibility of consumers.

CHAPTER SEVEN

*

The basics of the development of responsible consumer behavior

Today's consumption not only satisfies physiological or safety needs but has also in itself become an internalized need [Sułkowski 2012, p. 244]. People have become enslaved by global marketing because they have forgotten that it is they who hold the real power in the form of their disposable income. In the market they can "vote for" for those products which have been produced in accordance with the principles of social responsibility. They can do so autonomously, without succumbing to the influences of advertisements and fashion trends. Primarily, however, they can have an impact on what our world will look like in the future through their purchasing decisions [Hoppe and Karaszewski 2013, p. 102]. Responsible consumer behavior is the result of a deliberate selection process and of one's full awareness of what consequences a given choice will have on society as a whole and on the ecological future of the natural environment.

According to the adopted axiomatics of human nature, people are hedonists by definition. Is it possible then that consumers will behave in a socially responsible way? One can definitely answer "yes", but only if such actions will be the result of people's hedonistic inclinations. If such behavior brings one benefits (pleasure) or results from one's aversion to loss, i.e. (unpleasantness), then this type of behavior will most certainly occur. There is, however, at least one more precondition, i.e. such behavior must constitute a specific priority for a consumer as far as his/her hierarchy of needs is concerned. A human being who cannot fully satisfy his/her physiological needs will not be wondering whether to buy a product which is, for example, labeled A+++ for energy efficiency but which is completely beyond his/her financial capabilities. Is it possible that people living in a very poor country in which one is unable to feed one's children will start thinking in terms of socially responsible consumption as a priority?

Unfortunately no, because people in such countries will have entirely different priorities – which is completely understandable. It seems that it is most probable that responsible consumer behaviors occur when a society achieves a particular level of wealthiness and fulfillment of people's basic needs, i.e. a level at which the concepts of a benefit and pleasure become redefined.

The impact of a society's affluence on the level of responsible consumption (7.1)

Psychological research studies that were conducted at the turn of the new millennium on all continents have shown that one's well-being which is oriented toward a continuous increase in the consumption of goods and services leads to an impoverishment of interpersonal relations. People who are affected by such consumerism become less vigorous, less confident and less satisfied with their lives, family, friends as well as their income. They also become depressed more often, display abnormal social behaviors, adopt destructive attitudes, and have physical symptoms of stress [Welzer and Wiegandt 2011, p. 71]. In all societies, a rewarding job is an important part of one's personal happiness. Losing one's job is often associated with a sense of alienation and uselessness. However, the question arises about the amount of work that one carries out, the level of one's income and one's satisfaction with the possibility of purchasing more goods and services. Research shows that once the per capita GDP reaches a level of USD 20,000 (EUR 16,000), the percentage of the population that is satisfied with their lives remains at 60% and does not rise even if the GDP doubles. It turns out that after a particular level of well-being has been reached its further growth no longer matters, and things other than material goods begin to increase in importance. Studies that were carried out in 2007 in Germany showed that only 27% of society wanted to have a higher income, 59% of the respondents were happy with their income level and 10% would be willing to settle for a lower income. It seems that people are less and less satisfied with an increasing number of goods and that growing prosperity is increasingly less important for them; such an attitude also becomes stronger among the respondents as they get older. Only for people aged up to 30 is the percentage of those who want to become wealthier over 50%, while for people aged over 59 this percentage drops to 4% [Miegel 2011, p. 30-31]. Until people achieve this level of affluence, it is the price that mainly determines what goods they choose. The above-mentioned studies indicate that it is only after a certain level of wealthiness and consumption has been exceeded that people will begin to feel the desire to fulfill their needs indirectly connected with their hedonistic goals. Then people will begin to develop an aversion to the potential contamination of the natural environment and, consequently, to a possible deterioration in the quality of life in the future. It can be stated that then long-term, preventive thinking appears and the concept of a benefit (pleasure) is redefined. People become interested in the situations of other members of the community, which leads them to make conscious, socially responsible consumer decisions. Such decisions, however, which result from what the behaviorists would call a rationalization mechanism, are in fact a form of hedonism, i.e. they allow people to derive subjective pleasure from an illusory or rational concern for others. This is also a kind of "moral cleansing" which people engage in when they start to feel the need to justify all of their hedonistic actions before themselves and the need to "do" something for those who are not doing so well. Nonetheless, this is also when consumers start behaving in a socially responsible way.

Determinants of the growing level of socially responsible consumer behaviors (7.2)

In order to establish what factors determine socially responsible consumer behavior one should first ascertain the motivation behind such behavior. Apart from the appropriately high level of affluence, as has been established earlier, among such motivators are the following factors:

- people derive personal benefits from buying goods that conform to the idea of social responsibility or from socially and ecologically responsible behaviors (a reward),
- people are afraid that they may lose their health or that their living conditions may truly deteriorate (within a short and predictable time period) as a result of the lack of socially responsible behaviors (fear, punishment),
- such behavior is *en mode* because it is promoted by social or moral authorities (the desire to keep up with others, the need for belonging to a given social group),
- socially responsible products are manufactured by the most well-known brands (promotion),
- there is information asymmetry as regards the way in which purchased products are produced [Hoppe and Karaszewski 2013, p. 102].

All of the above elements of motivation are the result of what human nature is like. Each of the motivators is a reflection of a human being's hedonistic behavior and shows that people are only motivated by the prospect of achieving a benefit or by an aversion to being punished.

When analyzing the literature on the subject one can state that ethical, prosocial and pro-environmental consumption is a special kind of consumption. It is often referred to as higher-level consumption, which is an alternative to the "normal" type of consumption and a usually habitual way in which people buy goods and services on a daily basis. This type of consumption requires additional, and not necessarily monetary, costs. Consumers usually face information asymmetry, which causes them to look for additional information, for example, about the way in which the goods are manufactured, which is also counted toward the costs because it requires time, inventiveness and a search for access to information sources. A change in one's routines and habits related to shopping is another kind of cost that one incurs as a result of ethical consumption. According to many authors, this is a kind of psychological cost – consumers must accept the necessity of coping with huge amounts of information and analyzing it. Moreover, there can also be monetary costs; ecological products, rightly or wrongly so, are usually associated with a higher price. If during the production of goods all employee rights are respected and the natural environment is cared for, then the costs of such production are usually higher than when the goods are manufactured in an unethical way, which must somehow translate into a higher price of the end product.

The above list of costs is incomplete and this issue deserves to be analyzed separately and more thoroughly. What can also be concluded from this list is that if ethical consumption is to become a reality, the incurred costs will have to be compensated for by a particular benefit that one can derive from it. The question then arises as to what makes one decide to buy products that have been manufactured in accordance with the principles of CSR, i.e. what is the motivation behind this specific and often alternative type of consumption?

There are many papers in which the authors attempt to provide a systematic and exhaustive answer to this question. Brinkmann and Peattie

[2008] identified four main types of motivations which they refer to as combinations of private and social motives. These are:
- public motives – which are usually manifested in boycotting certain companies or goods that have been produced in an unethical way,
- private-social motives – an individual acts in an ethical way in order to be appreciated by a particular social group; conformist motivations cause altruistic actions,
- private-caring motives – an individual's ethical behavior is caused by his or her personal fears, for example, concerning the environment, and it is aimed to allay these fears,
- private-hedonistic motives – ethical consumption is a matter of fashion and a way to experience pleasure as well as to stand out in a crowd.

When analyzing the attitudes of consumers who bought fair trade products in Italy, Devitiis, D'Alessio and Maietta [2008] identified many kinds of benefits that could be derived from consumption and defined the following types of consumers who corresponded to these kinds of benefits: selfish ones, pleasure seeking and curious ones, ethical, ethical "hygienists" (those who are interested in activities for the benefit of future gains for society) as well as selfish "hygienists" (who act out of concern for their own health).

Szmigin and Carrigan [2006] systematized the attitudes of ethical consumers in a slightly different way. They studied the social dimension of ethical consumption with regard to the relationship between an individual decision-maker and the surrounding community. In this case the consumers' motivations range from hedonistic to highly empathic.

Many authors, however, have emphasized the complexity of motivations behind ethical consumption, which results from the diversity of benefits gained by consumers who take on particular attitudes and actions.

Also the causes of nominally prosocial behaviors may be different, i.e. altruistic and egoistic, which was highlighted by Devinney, Auger and Eckhardt [2010].

Karsaklian and Fee [2012] have proposed one of the most interesting approaches to this issue. With their aim of trying to understand and systematize the various kinds of motivation as well as to establish the possible extent to which these interact they have introduced a model in which they identified two dimensions along which all possible motivations behind ethical consumption can be extended.

The first of the dimensions defines the extent to which a given consumer's motivation depends on how other people perceive his or her ethical approach to consumption as well as on how much importance he or she attaches to the opinions of other members of the community. From this perspective, one's motivation may range from social to individual; therefore, it can be generated by norms that are imposed on from the outside or by those that are internally, individually defined. According to the authors, this issue boils down to whether it is more important for a consumer as to what others think of him/her (in the context of consumption, which is the point of reference here) or what he/she him-/herself believes is right or wrong. The first motivational dimension is related to the social, external effect of consumption or its lack.

The second dimension of motivation is connected with who, in the consumer's opinion, benefits from ethical consumption. Consumers might think that they are acting to the benefit of society, the natural environment or the public good by making ethical purchases, i.e. it is the society, the environment, etc. that derives benefits from such consumer choices. However, an opposite type of motivation is also often observed, i.e. a consumer him-/herself benefits from ethical consumption; for example, ecological products are often perceived to be "pure" and safe to one's health. Therefore, one will often be motivated to buy such goods out of concern for his or her own health and not out of concern for the environment. Then such a purchase also usually brings along real benefits to the natural environment, but here this fact has no influence on the very motivation behind such actions.

If all of the above-mentioned dimensions of motivation are taken into account one can define four main types of motivation for ethical consumption. Karsaklian and Fee present the following motivational categories:

- conformity,
- self-orientation,
- self-actualization,
- hedonism.

Conformity means that it is society that dictates the norms and benefits from consumer decisions. The only rational explanation as to why individuals take on such an attitude is that they have the need of belonging to a given group and of being accepted by a given community. Depending on the situation this may either bring further benefits or not.

Self-orientation is when a consumer accepts the rules of conduct that are imposed on by society and considers them important, but it is he/she him-/herself who benefits from an alternative lifestyle because this allows him/her to be different from others. Such a consumer wants to create an image of him-/herself as a unique individual who rises above mediocrity.

Self-actualization is the opposite of self-orientation. A consumer makes an individual decision to engage in ethical consumption for internal reasons (and perhaps also contrary to the views of society); however, his or her aim is to bring benefits to the entire community or the natural environment. These are altruistic motives which can, for example, be manifested in buying fair trade products and thus often provide benefits to impoverished people.

Hedonism is a type of motivation that is oriented toward one's personal gain regardless of what norms are favored by society. The ethical aspect of consumption increases the level of one's satisfaction as well as of the utility of the goods one has purchased. As the authors emphasize, the leading motive behind a consumer's behavior then is that he or she wants to feel good and not "do good".

The advantage of Karsaklian and Fee's typology is that it is clear and consistent with the various types of motivation that were described by other authors. These authors classify diverse motivation-related phenomena, which have been described by other researchers, as belonging to one of the four above-mentioned groups. The four types are general enough to encompass other, more detailed categories. This undoubtedly makes it possible to organize the chaos resulting from the diversity of categories of motivation that have been proposed by different authors. As a result, one can better understand which motivational factors are decisive in engaging oneself in ethical consumption and which ones are neglected. This is valuable information for theoreticians and practitioners alike. At the same time, attention should be paid to the fact that, actually, each of the above categories represents hedonistic motivation and only describes a different kind of a benefit, or pleasure, which is the true cause of such behavior.

Apart from one's personal motivation, what is also important is the legal system that is in force in a given community. Such a system may lay down many rules for manufacturing and taxing products that are to conform to the principle of social responsibility, which can then influence consumer decisions. This issue will be presented in more detail in one of the following sections.

A model of socially responsible consumer decisions (7.3)

In order to find out if responsible consumption can take place on a global scale, one should take a look at the process of making consumer decisions. This knowledge will make it possible to establish what elements of the process are of crucial importance to the expected choices.

Psychologically speaking, there are three kinds of consumer choices:
- repetitive, habitual,
- impulsive, unintended,
- conscious and reflective [Falkowski and Tyszka 2009, pp. 197-199].

Repetitive, habitual choices are usually related to daily necessities, i.e. when the decision-making process is very simplified. People usually buy the same products out of habit. As for impulsive, unintended choices, the stimulus-response mechanism is at work here, i.e. an impulse arises which causes a consumer to immediately make a purchase.

Only with regard to conscious and reflective choices does a consumer make a decision consciously, which usually takes place when one wants to buy goods and services of greater value. This kind of decision-making process, according to Loudon and Dell Bitta's classification, takes place in three situations:
1. The existing state of affairs changes, for example, when a consumer finds out that something broke or is worn out.
2. The desirable state of affairs changes – the objects one possesses have ceased to be fashionable or there are new products on the market which one does not yet have.

3. Both the existing and the desirable state of affairs change – this is a combination of the first two situations, i.e. something is worn out or broke, and at the same time something more modern has appeared on the market.

Carrington, Neville and Whitwell's [2010] article was the first to present a dynamic model of progression from an intention to consumption while taking into account inconsistencies that occur in the meantime. The authors analyzed the subsequent stages of the decision-making process and pointed to factors that can have an influence on all of its possible outcomes.

This process begins the moment that **intentions** are formed. These shape the specific, future decisions of consumers. Motivational factors that determine consumers' ethical intentions were dealt with in the previous section, whereas in Carrington, Neville and Whitwell's paper it is the decision-maker that is a starting point for an analysis.

The **implementation of intentions** is the next stage. This is when an ethical consumer's views and intentions translate into real decisions that are made in particular situations. This process takes on the form of strategies. The implementation of intentions allows one to put (not necessarily final) intentions into action, protects one's intentions against different types of external interference and is crucial if one wants to change his/her old consumption habits. This helps one develop patterns of behavior that express his or her individual beliefs. The level of implementing a consumer's intentions may be different; if this process has not started yet, then the previously formed intentions fall at the first hurdle, i.e. due to attractive promotions, a massive amount of information, alternative offers, etc. Generally speaking, the higher the level of implementation of a consumer's intentions, the greater the chance that the intention-behavior gap will narrow, i.e. that the difference between one's intentions as well as declaration and actual behaviors will become smaller. The authors do not specify, however, what causes intentions to be implemented and what the level of such implementation depends on. This is what these authors did, to a certain extent, in their paper dated 2012 which was a continuation of their former article and which will be discussed later in this book. One may, however, wonder if this is not some sort of battle between the hedonistic unconscious and the consciousness which develops in the socialization process.

The implementation of intentions itself is not the final factor transforming intentions into consumption. Carrington, Neville and Whitwell noticed two other important factors: behavioral control and the situational context.

The concept of **behavioral control** describes an individual's ability to control his/her actions and determines the level of this control. This is another factor that leads to the narrowing of the intention-behavior gap.

The **situational context** refers to the multitude of temporary factors that influence consumer behavior. In their article these authors refer to Belk's [1975] paper which deals with the impact that the situational context has on consumer behavior in general without taking into account its social, economic, or ethical aspects. Belk identified five main factors that make up the situational context:
- the physical surroundings of the buyer, i.e. the physical possibility of comparing goods' prices and characteristics and of assessing the way they are displayed on a store shelf,
- the social surroundings of the buyer, i.e. the presence of other people when one is doing one's shopping, as well as their influence and interactions,

- time perspective, i.e. the temporal aspects of making purchases, such as the time of day, time limitations, etc.,
- the task's definition, which depends on one's purpose of being in a store; i.e. whether it concerns buying something, collecting information, or making a preselection,
- the preceding state of affairs, which is related to temporary states and conditions that first did not have any connection with a given purchase but which have been introduced into this situation by the consumer; these might be temporary moods such as excitement, fear, etc. as well as other kinds of factors (the amount of money one has at a given moment, sickness, etc.).

All of these factors influence the spur-of-the-moment decisions that are made by consumers with regard to ethical consumption; however, as the authors noticed, such factors were omitted from the analyses that have been carried out to date. The impact that such factors have on the intention-behavior gap is, however, ambiguous; it can be either positive or negative, which is a particularly important observation with respect to ethical consumption. Devinney, Auger and Eckhardt [2012] describe an experiment in which they caused an increase in the demand for fair trade coffee from 1% to 70% by manipulating the context of a simulated sale of this product and its alternative types.

By presenting their model of progressing from intention to consumption, Carrington, Neville and Whitwell draw attention to the interdependence of all of these factors and to their distribution over time. A decision is implemented before behavioral control and situational context come into play. The last two factors may step in simultaneously or in any other order, depending on the situation. However, the situational context is regarded as a set of short-term and, generally speaking, temporally unstable elements, whereas behavioral control is a relatively stable factor because it expresses one's ability to be somewhat consistent in one's actions. In addition, the situational context has a local impact, for example, in a store, whereas behavioral control extends its influence beyond the place of purchase.

In their next article the above-mentioned authors elaborated their model of how intentions translate into actual consumer behaviors. This is a dynamic model and, as previously, an intention and the prioritization of ethical values related to consumption form its basis, i.e. it is important whether such values are primary or secondary for the consumer. Integration of these values into the shopping mode is the next stage of the decision-making process. This stage may be systematic and planned, it may be characterized by a tendency to sacrifice or it may be just the opposite. Depending on the type and level of such integration, the process reaches the next stage, i.e. of putting into practice the variables that have been mentioned before by engaging in particular behavior when purchasing goods. At this stage, however, behaviors may be well-thought over, quick or spontaneous, or requiring effort. Each set of values of the above-mentioned variables produces one of the two possible outcomes, i.e. the purchase of goods may reflect a consumer's intentions correctly or incorrectly. If the latter happens, then there is the intention-behavior gap. The model which has been described systematizes the causes of this discrepancy, thus making it easier to understand this phenomenon; it can also be useful for companies that wish to offer their products to the ethically minded consumer.

These reflections definitely do not solve the problem related to the possibility of developing socially responsible consumption patterns as a long-lasting, mass, social phenomenon. However, by referring to the preceding sections, one can certainly state that creating motivators that would be compatible with hedonistic human nature, i.e. related to the pursuit of a benefit (pleasure) and an aversion to unpleasantness, is a prerequisite for the emergence of this phenomenon. Who can create such motivators?

Such motivators should be developed by those who have the highest stake in promoting socially responsible consumption, i.e. businesses that manufacture products according to the principle of social responsibility, for obvious reasons, as well as state institutions whose task it is to protect the environment or to supervise the observance of the law. The possible ways in which they can act in order to promote socially responsible consumption will be discussed in the following parts of this book.

CHAPTER EIGHT
*
Consumer social responsibility – ConSR

The discussion on consumer social responsibility (ConSR) should be commenced by introducing this concept's definitions, which will be presented based on a review of the relevant literature.

According to the first definition, consumer social responsibility (ConSR) in its broadest sense means making conscious and wise consumer choices based on one's personal moral beliefs. A responsible consumer should mainly take into account the social aspect of products and the processes of the company that has manufactured the products. Such behavior is in part responsible for the growing importance of ethical and social factors for businesses.

ConSR can be manifested in:

- taking part in specific activities such as providing financial support or expressing one's readiness to join protests against or boycotts of particular products or companies,
- making conscious decisions to purchase or refuse to purchase some products,
- giving one's opinion in surveys or participating in other forms of market research concerning the products that one buys [Devinney et al. 2006, p. 3].

According to the second definition, social and ecological responsibility of consumers (ConSR) refers to the behaviors of consumers who consciously choose goods and services that are manufactured by those businesses which carry out both strategic and operational activities in accordance with the principles of corporate social responsibility. Socially and ecologically responsible consumer behaviors are related to the processes of buying products of all categories, from goods that satisfy people's basic physiological needs to luxury goods and those which allow them to meet their higher-order needs. In order for this responsibility to become permanently entrenched in society, buyers should develop high social and ecological awareness and be fully conscious of what consequences their choices might have on all members of the community they live in as well as on the ecological future of the natural environment on earth [Cyfert and Hoppe 2011, pp. 13-21].

The concept of ConSR is broader than that of responsible consumption; it is also connected with the rules for how to use the goods one has bought and what to do with them after they have been used. A set of behaviors which are encompassed by this concept shed some light on this issue. For the sake of clarity these behaviors have been divided into social and ecological ones. Among the social behaviors are primarily the following:

- buying goods that have been produced in accordance with the conception of corporate social responsibility,
- purchasing goods that have been produced according to the principle of fair trade,
- not buying counterfeit goods (respecting intellectual property),
- buying such an amount of food that one will definitely be able to eat,
- buying cosmetic products which have not been tested on animals,
- making purchasing decisions in a conscious, non-habitual way;

whereas among ecological behaviors there are:

- sorting waste and disposing of hazardous waste in such a way which will ensure that it does not pollute the environment,
- buying energy- and material-efficient appliances,
- using renewable energy sources,

- purchasing goods that will have the lowest negative impact on the environment,
- buying goods that have been produced in an environmentally friendly way,
- purchasing products that are made from recycled material as well as products that can be 100% recycled,
- buying high-quality products with long life cycles [Dudziński, Hoppe and Karaszewski 2012].

The influence of different socio-economic phenomena on ConSR, and vice versa, will be analyzed in the next part of this chapter.

Consumer social responsibility in the CSR system (8.1)

When businesses aim to meet the requirements of interest groups that not only expect activities to be directed toward generating profit but also expect proper care of the surroundings, these businesses increasingly more often implement the objectives of corporate social responsibility (CSR). In most cases, companies declaring that they have implemented CSR treat this idea more as a trend than a real desire to redesign their business model. There is, however, a large group of business entities that take objectives connected with social and ecological responsibility very seriously. The problem is that if their products are not accepted by consumers, these companies will not have a chance of gaining a durable competitive advantage. This means that the issue of developing the social and ecological responsibility of consumers is becoming one of the crucial factors that determine successful implementation of CSR [Cyfert and Hoppe 2011].

In J. Gustafson's opinion [2007, pp. 190-193], putting the idea of corporate social responsibility into practice means that the following rules must be accepted:

- One must be sensitive to matters that have an impact on the lives of the people one works with.
- One must understand the conditions in which society lives in order to be able to exert a positive influence on this society.
- One should consider the social consequences of financial and business decisions on large groups of voters, stakeholders, and the environment.
- One should be aware not only of what a given company manufactures, but also how it manufactures its products.

There is a kind of interdependence between ConSR and CSR. ConSR will lose its *raison d'être* without CSR, and CSR will have no chance of developing without ConSR. It is CSR, however, that must come into being first and must take this risk. The concept of CSR is one of the possible organizational strategies for gaining a competitive advantage, but it is unlikely that society will achieve a high level of ConSR given a human being's hedonistic nature, as was established earlier.

Businesses which act in accordance with the principles of CSR often make the following *a priori* assumptions without analyzing consumers' attitudes in detail:

- Consumers living in the vicinity of the companies appreciate their prosocial and pro-environmental activity.
- Consumers are able to consciously choose products and services offered by businesses that act according to the principles of CSR.
- Consumers have the appropriate ecological awareness and social sensitivity, which determines what kind of products and services they choose.

If the above assumptions are accepted without prior analysis of the real state of affairs, then this might turn out to be a serious mistake in the design of a business model's assumptions, as management practice has shown. This, in turn, may result in the inability to achieve a durable competitive advantage in the best-case scenario and in a company's bankruptcy in the worst-case scenario [Cyfert and Hoppe 2011].

Given the previous assertions about the possibility of developing ConSR, businesses should first start introducing the conception of CSR in societies that have reached an appropriate level of affluence. One should also very carefully study the rules of culture and the legal system in a given market as these may either support or hinder ConSR's development. One should also remember that businesses are managed by leaders or collective bodies that are made up of people who are hedonists by nature. Is engaging stakeholders in the operational management of a company not some kind of reciprocity? Is this not the real motive behind the idea of CSR? Does the concept of social responsibility not hide people's hedonistic nature, which then makes companies expect reciprocity from stakeholders as well as understanding if any negligence or unethical behavior takes place?

In my opinion, the idea of CSR should be introduced into a company's organization by using an emergent strategy which is continuously adjusted to the changing environment. In addition, one can hardly agree with the idea of engaging all stakeholders in the creation of operational rules due to the evident conflict of interests of different groups of influence. Such a situation could lead to a kind of anarchy as well as to making decisions that would not be the most advantageous to a given business; companies might also need to limit themselves to meeting the expectations of only some of their stakeholders, which could cause unnecessary conflicts. One should rather adhere to the principle of social responsibility which entails adjusting the activity of a business to the essence of the idea of sustainable development, which would, however, be formulated by the managers, i.e. those who have the greatest knowledge concerning all of their company's processes as well as the possible ways of changing or adapting them to the new concept. A given company's leaders would play the main role in objectively establishing which solutions are the most advantageous for all stakeholders; after all it is the leaders of a business who bear full responsibility for its performance.

Bolesław Rok [2013] gives an example of a very interesting opinion on this matter. He quotes Peter Drucker, who claimed that businesses will not adhere to the principles of social responsibility if this adherence is not in their own interest, i.e. if they are not able to translate such activities into a prospect of gain. Does this not further confirm that the model of human nature which has been presented here is correct?

International organizations and state institutions are able to eliminate the risk connected with implementing the concept of CSR by businesses because they can shape the systems of both international and national laws so that these systems support CSR and, most of all, will cause the level of consumer social responsibility to rise by using proper positive and negative reinforcements. It seems that all such activities should be adapted to the nature of human behaviors which are based on the pursuit of pleasure, i.e. a benefit, and an aversion to risk, i.e. unpleasantness. This issue will be dealt with more extensively in the following parts of this chapter.

ConSR vs sustainable development (8.2)

The 'socially responsible consumer' is a new concept which is, however, gaining in importance. This is because society has been receiving information about the consequences of unsustainable development for over a decade. It is always emphasized that responsibility for the natural environment is our common cause, which is evidenced by the currently observed weather anomalies that result from people's irresponsible behaviors. The definitions of sustainable development which are presented below clearly confirm how important consumer social responsibility is.

One of the first such definitions was formulated in 1987; it was published as part of a report of the UN World Commission on Environment and Development:

> *Sustainable development is development that meets the needs of the present without compromising the ability of future generations to meet their own needs.*

There are many similar definitions of this concept in the literature; these are, for example, the following: sustainable development is socio-economic development that makes it possible to satisfy the basic needs of all humanity on a global scale and at the same time does not limit the ability of future generations to satisfy their needs [Seidl and Zahrnt 2010, p. 25]. The primary objective of sustainable development is to fairly and evenly distribute happiness among all people of the present generation and those of many future generations [Jäger 2010, p. 202]. The idea of self-restraint is connected with sustainable development. This concept refers to everyday consumer behaviors; it is not about being ascetic but about leading such a lifestyle that will allow future generations to have living standards that will not be worse than ours. Self-restraint is to lead one to consciously purchase goods which one needs in order to achieve one's expected standard of living but also to choose goods that are produced in accordance with the principles of sustainable development and to buy such an amount of these goods which is truly needed [Weizsäcker, Hargroves and Smith 2010, pp. 355-370].

In the 1987 report which was cited above it was considered a matter of the utmost importance that activities be undertaken in the three following domains:

- economic growth and an equitable distribution of benefits – the aim is to achieve "responsible", long-term development which will be experienced by all nations and communities, but in order for this to become a reality one must adopt an integrated approach to today's interconnected global economic systems;
- conservation of natural resources and the environment – if we want to preserve our environmental heritage and natural resources for future generations it is necessary that economically rational solutions be developed which will reduce resource consumption, stop environmental pollution and save natural ecosystems;
- social development – people all over the world require jobs, food, education, energy, health care, water and sanitation systems. In response to these needs the international community must make every effort to prevent the depletion of cultural richness and social diversity as well as to allow all members of societies to have means enabling them to shape their own future [From a report of the UN World Commission on Environment and Development: *Our Common Future*, 1987].

During the Earth Summit that was held in 1992 in Rio de Janeiro, one of the most important documents related to the topic of sustainable development was drawn up, i.e. *Agenda 21*. This document contains, for example, the following statement:

> Humanity stands at a defining moment in history. We are confronted with a perpetuation of disparities between and within nations, a worsening of poverty, hunger, ill health and illiteracy, and the continuing deterioration of the ecosystems on which we depend for our well-being.

as well as a proposal to change our strategy in the future:

> New ways of investing in the future are necessary if we are to achieve global sustainable development in the twenty-first century. The recommendations concern issues ranging from new teaching methods to new methods of using raw materials and participating in the creation of a sustainable economy. *Agenda 21* aims to lead us toward a safe and just world in which all living beings will be able to retain their dignity (own translation).

The next Earth Summit in Rio de Janeiro, called *Rio +20*, was held in June 2012. During the 20 years that had passed from the previous meeting the world population had grown by 1.5 billion to nearly 7 billion, which was accompanied by an increase in the number of global issues, such as: extreme poverty that affects every fifth person; the fact that 2.5 billion people live in primitive conditions and have no access to basic sanitary facilities; and the rising amount of greenhouse gas emissions which threaten to destroy one-third of all species living on earth.

Sustainable development is one of the areas of interest of many international organizations; for example:

- The United Nations Environment Programme (UNEP),
- The United Nations Development Programme (UNDP),
- institutions of the European Union:
  - The European Parliament,
  - The European Commission,
  - The European Economic and Social Committee.

The idea of sustainable development is also an important element of the international legal system. The most important international legal documents dealing with the issue of sustainable development are:

- *Agenda 21*,
- *The UNECE Convention on Access to Information, Public Participation in Decision-making and Access to Justice in Environmental Matters (The Aarhus Convention)*.

The idea of sustainable development is also a part of the legal systems of many countries in the world. In Poland it is mentioned in Article 5 of the Constitution:

> The Republic of Poland shall safeguard the independence and integrity of its territory and ensure the freedoms and human rights as well as rights of the citizens, and the security of the citizens; it shall also safeguard national heritage and ensure the protection of the natural environment pursuant to the principles of sustainable development.

From all of the principles of sustainable development that have been cited here it can be clearly concluded that attaining such development is inextricably linked to the concepts CSR and ConSR. Theoretically speaking, this means that the concept of CSR should have been in use as an organizational strategy all over the world for a long time. If so many international organizations and almost all countries of the world decided to support the idea of sustainable development then the conditions for conducting responsible business activity should be excellent. Unfortunately, the reality is somewhat different and, in practice, sustainable development is very often just an empty slogan; e.g. in Poland, Article 5 of the Constitution is not always complied with. Many provisions of the law, in particular tax law, are inconsistent with the Polish Constitution. How else, for example, could one interpret the fact that the amount of excise duty on cars depends on a given car's engine capacity and not on the quantity of its exhaust gases? It turns out that political populism and government revenue are more important than sustainable development.

This lack of compatibility of legal systems and the idea of sustainable development as well as the lack of legal tools that would support the emergence of such development result in a low level of social responsibility among consumers. One can hardly expect that society will start dealing with this important problem itself if people notice how neglected it is by state authorities – this is not in our human nature. It is urgent that the state reorganize the legal system by making it consistent with the principles of sustainable development and by supporting desirable social behaviors.

The influence of information asymmetry on the level of ConSR (8.3)

The issue of information asymmetry was described in more detail in Chapter Two (2.3). It would be, however, worthwhile to once again mention that it was George Akerlof, Michael Spence and Joseph Stiglitz who analyzed this phenomenon and who received the Nobel Prize for their research studies on this topic. As has been shown, this is a widespread phenomenon which affects many spheres of social life. Information asymmetry is very important from the perspective of consumer social responsibility. There is no chance whatsoever that consumers who are not able to obtain reliable information about the products they purchase will act in a responsible way. One cannot, therefore, expect that ConSR will develop if businesses do not introduce any changes. There will be no corporate social responsibility for as long as entrepreneurs fail to provide reliable information to consumers about all aspects of the products they manufacture. From the practices of businesses that are now taking place one may conclude that they are not trying to deal with this problem. It seems that most companies are not willing to discuss all of their production processes or the social and ecological aspects of their activity. This undoubtedly constitutes a large barrier to the development of consumer social responsibility. In addition, attention should be paid to the fact that consumers have increasingly less confidence in the quality of information that is provided by businesses. If this does not change quickly, one can assume that it might be impossible for companies to regain consumers' trust and earn a good reputation in the future.

The role of the state in creating socially responsible consumer behavior (8.4)

As was indicated in the previous sections, it is a matter of urgency that the state support the development of socially responsible behavior. The state has a wide range of opportunities it can use to influence the market and to initiate socially responsible consumer behaviors. Among the most important tools that the state can use are [Weizsäcker, Hargroves and Smith 2010, p. 264]:

- tradable emission permits,
- tradable resource (raw material) allocations,
- product charges and taxes on hazardous products,
- fees and taxes on emissions of harmful substances,
- a tax on minerals,
- a tax reform involving tax burdens on undesirable behaviors toward the environment and tax incentives for desirable behaviors,
- a deposit-refund system which supports the management of resource-recirculating packaging,
- subsidies for environmental protection,
- environmental responsibility which requires that harm which has been done to the natural environment be compensated for,
- financial guarantees for desirable innovations,
- establishing compulsory provisions with the aim of restoring contaminated sites to their original state,
- a progressive tax on electricity consumption,
- subsidies for the production of energy from renewable sources.

The idea of taxing the consumption of common goods is not new – it was first proposed by Arthur Pigou[3]. However, it is important that the above-mentioned tax-related proposals not increase the overall tax burden on society and that they be used to reduce other encumbrances, such as labor costs. Such moves should have a positive influence on those areas which are expected to develop. The amounts of these taxes should be positively correlated with an economy's growing resource and energy efficiency so that they do not lead to higher inflation [Hoppe 2013].

The state's activities should be compatible with the AMHHB model. Unfortunately, it would not be legitimate to assume that society will achieve a high level of social responsibility without external support. This is not in our human nature, which is visible in the way consumers behave.

Bolesław Rok [2013] states that rules for supporting the development of CSR should be introduced at the level of the European Union. He believes that the following assertions, among others, should form the basis of economic and social policy:

- Creating better conditions for implementing the principles of corporate social responsibility and active promotion of good practices is an important factor in increasing an economy's potential for development. What is essential is a favorable social climate as well as a specific ethical infrastructure both within a business organization and in its surroundings.

- Public administration at all levels of government should, while carrying out its tasks, take into greater account the creation of conditions for sustainable development and responsible competitiveness.

---

[3] Arthur Cecil Pigou (1877-1959) – a British economist and precursor of neoclassical welfare economics.

- Economically viable and jointly developed instruments of supporting CSR should be used so as to encourage businesses to engage in socially responsible behaviors; also, the existing legal regulations should be modified [Rok 2013, p. 56].

Unfortunately, only by inspecting the legal regulations on public procurement that are being used by Polish public administrative bodies and by observing the daily reality in which the price is the only criterion that is being used in the public procurement of goods and services, can one definitely state that we are still very far from adopting desirable solutions. In my opinion, procedures for supporting the ideas of sustainable development and corporate social responsibility should primarily be introduced at the local level of the state's administrative structure.

One can hardly expect large-scale development of the concept of CSR in companies without state assistance. Fulfilling the obligations that were undertaken during the 1992 Earth Summit turned out to be a fiasco. The state can, most of all, adjust the legal system in such a way as to base it on positive reinforcements (benefits) that one would obtain in return for socially responsible behavior. The appropriate tax law that would encourage people to buy products which have been manufactured in accordance with the conception of CSR would play an important role in this process. A no less important task for the state would be to educate people on a large scale about the consequences of their consumer decisions and the way in which they use particular products. Waste management that is consistent with the idea of a sustainable domestic economy could be another domain of the state's activity.

However, if such activity is to make sense, appropriate legislation should be implemented in all countries of the world and it should be controlled by international organizations. Is this possible? Unfortunately, given the previous experiences with implementing the idea of sustainable development in the world, one cannot be so optimistic.

There is one more issue that seems to be important for the future development of ConSR, i.e. the proposed model of a hedonistic human being. If it were to become accepted and recognized as consistent with reality, then this model would contribute to a change in the thinking about the possibility of introducing other tools for influencing social behaviors. I am certainly in favor of adjusting all of the tools currently being used to human nature and in accordance with AMHHB; these tools are mainly legal systems that are based on positive reinforcements.

The issue of measuring ConSR will be further discussed along with the methodological problems that are associated with such research.

Research problems related to ConSR – the mind-behavior gap (8.5)

Large groups of respondents stated in numerous surveys that ethical and ecological values were important to them as far as the process of consumption was concerned. However, market research has shown that noble intentions hardly translate into real spending. This phenomenon is referred to as the mind-behavior gap [Carrigan and Attalla 2001, Nicholls and Lee 2006, Auger and Devinney 2007]. Cowe and Williams [2000] and Futerra [2005] describe this relation in terms of the 30:3 proportion. The research studies they carried out showed that about 30 percent of respondents stated that they cared about ethical values in relation to consumption, while only three percent of their purchases reflected these intentions.

Auger and Devinney [2007] argued that this gap can partially be explained by the fact that imperfect methods were used to study consumers' attitudes. Their research studies showed that the traditional survey methods were inadequate for studying ethical consumption because they caused an artificial increase, or "inflation", of declared prosocial attitudes. The results that were obtained by conducting traditional surveys were a mixture of people's true beliefs as well as preferences and false information about a given topic. Moreover, a simple psychological mechanism is at work here that causes people who are directly questioned about ethical issues to give positive, politically correct and socially accepted answers – which does not cost them much. Cowe and Williams [2000] as well as Clavin and Lewis [2005] also emphasized that such a phenomenon exists and they stressed its importance. It can be concluded from Auger and Devinney's research that one should pay particular attention to what tools are selected and how they are constructed if social attitudes of consumers are to be studied. The results of surveys concerning ethical consumer behaviors turn out to be highly sensitive to the very way in which these surveys are conducted.

The attitude-intention gap is a fact; therefore, the most important problem that researchers are faced with is that they must understand and explain the phenomenon of this gap, i.e. its causes, mechanics and dynamics. This is vital both for theoretical and practical reasons. Companies that launch goods which have been produced with care for the natural environment and with respect for ethical matters cannot operate without reliable feedback on the demand for such goods. As the above-mentioned research studies have shown, the surveys that are usually used can be very misleading. It is therefore crucial and essential that one understand the phenomenon of the intention-behavior gap itself and identify the factors that hinder ethical consumption.

Eckhardt, Belk and Devinney [2010] point to the difference in costs, among other things. It costs people nothing to declare that their attitudes are prosocial or pro-environmental, whereas ethical consumption is always connected with the necessity of incurring certain costs. Such costs might, certainly, be monetary if particular products are more expensive, but these could also be different kinds of costs. One must often devote time and energy to finding a given product and, also, give up habits of convenience related to shopping. If one wants to break with an old shopping habit, one must also incur some psychological costs which are difficult to measure but which undoubtedly exist. Many authors [Bray, Johns and Kilburn 2011] emphasize that the shopping habits people have previously developed are difficult to overcome and that they constitute one of the main obstacles to popularizing ethical consumption.

Eckhardt, Belk and Devinney [2010] have attempted to systematize the arguments that consumers use to justify the fact that they do not take into account ethical aspects when making consumer decisions. Based on interviews with 160 people coming from eight countries, the researchers identified three main types of such justification:

- economic rationalization,
- institutional dependency,
- developmental realism.

Economic rationalization of consumption is based on rational arguments referring to utility which is most influenced by the costs a consumer incurs. Consumers stress the role of price as the most decisive factor in choosing goods. As for a cost-benefit analysis, it should be noted that such an approach is rational if and only if goods that have been produced in an ethical or ecological way do not represent a higher value for consumers. If the benefit that can be derived from both kinds of goods is the same then it is certainly better to buy cheaper products. Such an analysis is, however, only true for consumers who do not notice the ethical aspects of consumption – their arguments will be purely economic.

According to a belief based on **institutional dependency**, concern for the environment and employee rights, etc. should be the domain of governments as well as institutions established by those governments for this purpose, whereas consumers' individual decisions are of secondary importance. From this assumption follows the rule that if certain products or practices connected with manufacturing those products are legally allowed by the authorities, then consumers do not have to question the legitimacy of such products even though they are produced in an unethical way. Interestingly, researchers have observed that many respondents also count companies and advertising agencies among the above-mentioned institutions which are to take care of ethical matters through top-down regulations, thereby shifting responsibility onto the authorities and institutions. It seems that such an attitude is partly based on conformism and partly on a feeling that the individual has hardly any or no influence at all on ecology, employee rights, etc.; many respondents said directly that if these problems were to be solved effectively, they should be dealt with by institutions and the legal system.

Developmental realism describes the third of the common ways in which consumers justify their behaviors. According to this belief, poor working conditions, low wages or lack of respect for the natural environment as well as intellectual property are part of a natural, economically enforced standard practice at a certain stage of economic development in some (usually developing) countries. The above arguments are similar to those used when people economically rationalize consumption, but these are presented from a macroeconomic perspective. Respondents stressed that they could not afford to take ethical matters into account because they were too poor for this, both as individuals and as society as a whole. Low wages result from the situation in a given economy as well as the existing market equilibrium. This is when, typically, buying fake branded goods is a socially accepted practice.

The analysis carried out by Eckhardt, Belk and Devinney systematizes the ways in which consumers justify and rationalize their behaviors and it explains why the kind of consumption they engage in does not reflect ethical principles, regardless of whether they profess such principles or not. This is why this analysis cannot fully explain the phenomenon of the intention-behavior gap.

Bray, Johns and Kilburn [2011] identified eight factors that disrupt the continuity between consumers' views and intentions and their actual behavior. These are:

- consumers' sensitivity to price – this factor is analogous to economic rationalization as described by Eckhardt, Belk and Devinney;
- personal experience – consumers cannot see the positive influence of their decisions and expenditure; it has been observed that people's negative reactions to bad news are strong and their positive reactions to good news about the final results of charitable activity are weak;
- ethical duty – ethical consumption is perceived as a way to salve one's conscience but at the same time people do not have faith in the effectiveness of such actions;
- lack of information – respondents mention that there is a lack of adequate knowledge on the products they purchase, on the conditions in which these products are produced and the impact these products have on the environment;
- perception of quality – some consumers regard fair trade products as being of lower quality; this does not have to result from their experience but from their habitual perceptions of certain notions about the world;
- inertia associated with shopping – patterns, customs and habits that lead one to buy particular brands of products as well as loyalty toward specific companies are factors that strongly prevent one from changing one's ways;
- cynicism – respondents think that the ethical or ecological images of certain companies and goods are only marketing gimmicks which are aimed at attracting consumers' attention and making a given company stand out among its competitors on the market. It was noticed that such an attitude was usually connected with a lack of information about the benefits that one might derive from ethical consumption and with exaggerated information about unethical practices;

- guilt – results from one's earlier attitude to consumption which was not very ethical; paradoxically, this feeling, when suppressed, is sometimes manifested as self-justification and doubts as to whether ethical consumption has any real positive effects.

The above list of factors is consistent with the results of previous studies on this topic and, in general, confirms and puts these results in order [Carrigan and Attalla 2001, Nicholls and Lee 2006]; although the authors point out that the list might be incomplete and the topic may require further research.

This summary of factors hindering ethical consumption and the related analysis undoubtedly make it easier to understand the phenomenon of the intention-behavior gap but they have no predictive value because they do not constitute a comprehensive model of a transition from intentions to their actual implementation. The assumption of most of the existing models describing the consumption-related decision-making process which takes ethical norms into account is that the intentions which have been formed are directly implemented through consumer behaviors [Shaw and Shui 2002, Vermeir and Verbeke 2007, Arvola et al. 2008]. In practice, this means that the intention-behavior gap is omitted.

Knowledge about this phenomenon is of considerable importance for the world of science and economic practice. It can definitely be concluded that previous studies on consumer behavior which were based on survey methods were fraught with high levels of error. Therefore, there is a methodological gap in the research which has to be filled in by carrying out quantitative research on consumer behavior. One such new research method is proposed in the article: Dudziński P., Gotowska M., Hoppe G., Jakubczak A., Karaszewski R., 2013, *Obiektywna metoda pomiaru poziomu społecznej i ekologicznej odpowiedzialności konsumentów (ConSR)* ["An objective method for measuring the level of social and ecological responsibility of consumers (ConSR)"], Ekonomia i Środowisko [*Economics and the Environment*], no. 3, pp. 272-291.

Measuring the level of ConSR – the results of own research (8.6)

In 2013 a research team, of which I was a member, carried out survey research under the supervision of Professor Robert Karaszewski, PhD. This survey was aimed to establish the level of consumer social responsibility. The group of respondents was a purposive sample and comprised families of students of the Nicolaus Copernicus University in Toruń and the University of Technology and Life Sciences in Bydgoszcz, Poland. The study sample consisted of 1,511 individuals (in families), which made it possible to generalize the results to the entire population that this group belonged to. The survey questionnaire is presented in Annex 1. When analyzing the obtained results one should, however, remember about the problem related to the intention-behavior gap, which should be taken into consideration when drawing conclusions.

Methodology

A survey method was used to study the purposive sample in order to establish the level of ConSR; the participants were asked to fill out the survey questionnaire (Annex 1) together with the other members of their households. A total of 1,511 completed questionnaires were obtained and the answers were aggregated.

Sample characteristics:

The respondents were characterized on the basis of classification questions.

Sex	
Female	62%
Male	37%
Age	
Under 18 years old	2%
18-30 years old	52%
31-45 years old	20%
46-65 years old	21%
66 years old and older	5%
Education (completed)	
Elementary school	2%
Junior high school	2%
Basic vocational school	12%
High school	48%

Higher education (including bachelor's and engineer's degrees)	36%
Place of residence	
Town/city – multi-family residential buildings	44%
Town/city – single-family buildings	21%
Rural areas	34%
Livelihood	
Student	34%
Currently unemployed	4%
Earned income	52%
Income from retirement pension/other kinds of pension (disability)	10%
Number of persons in the household	
1	5%
2	17%
3	25%
4	31%
5	0%
Over 5	22%

Monthly net income	
Below PLN 1,000 (approx. USD 326) per month	13%
From PLN 1,000 to 2,500 (approx. USD 326-814) per month	42%
From PLN 2,500 to 5,000 (approx. USD 814-1,628) per month	32%
Over PLN 5,000 (approx. USD 1,628) per month	12%
No answer	1%

All of the answers should be treated as data about the individuals filling out the survey questionnaire, which means they were not only students. As can be concluded from the results, the questionnaires were filled out in equal parts by the heads of the families and students, which is evident from the respondents' answers concerning age (52% of the individuals were aged 18-30) as well as livelihood (52% derived their income from work).

After having analyzed the respondents' personal date, one may state that the distribution of answers indicates that the group is highly representative of the entire society, which makes it somewhat possible to generalize the research results to the whole community. This means that it is very likely that the citizens of Poland have characteristics that are similar to those of the respondents.

Analysis of the level of ConSR based on the research results

The results of the research study are presented below in graphical form along with an analysis.

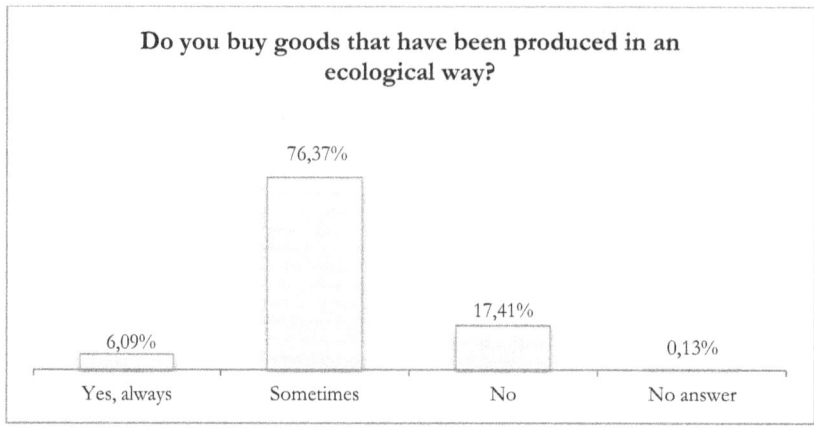

Fig. 8.6.1. Graphical representation of responses to question no. 1.

Answers to question no. 1 show that an ecological way of manufacturing products only motivates a small number of respondents (6%) to buy such products. A compilation of these responses indicates a low level of ConSR in the sample. When one takes into account the problems related to the intention-behavior gap, it can be assumed that most of the "sometimes" responses are declarative.

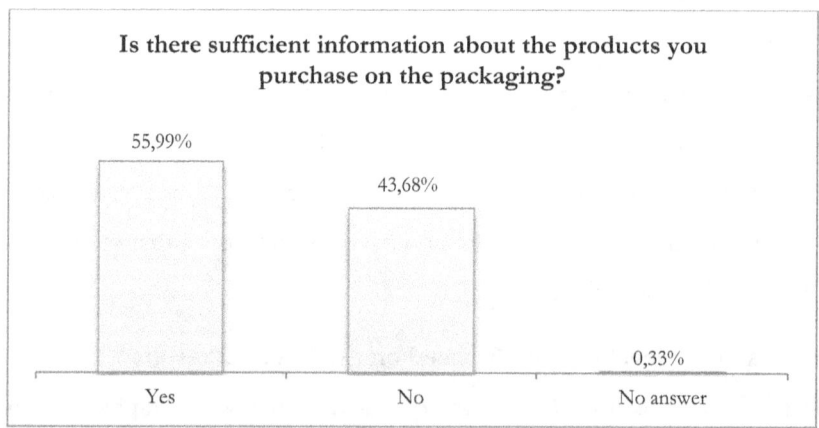

Fig. 8.6.2. Graphical representation of responses to question no. 2.

Because the information that is provided on product labels is, in reality, not sufficient enough to allow consumers to make a socially responsible choice and 56% of the respondents consider such information to be sufficient, the level of ConSR in the sample is low.

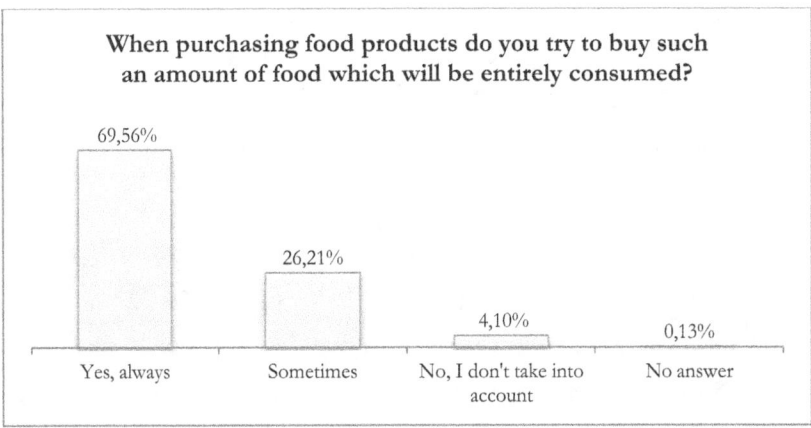

Fig. 8.6.3. Graphical representation of responses to question no. 5.

An analysis of the answers to the above question in combination with sample characteristics indicates that the respondents are frugal when it comes to food products, especially as only 12% of them belong to the wealthiest of the groups. However, the fact that 69.5% of the respondents answered "yes, always" cannot be treated as indicative of socially responsible behavior.

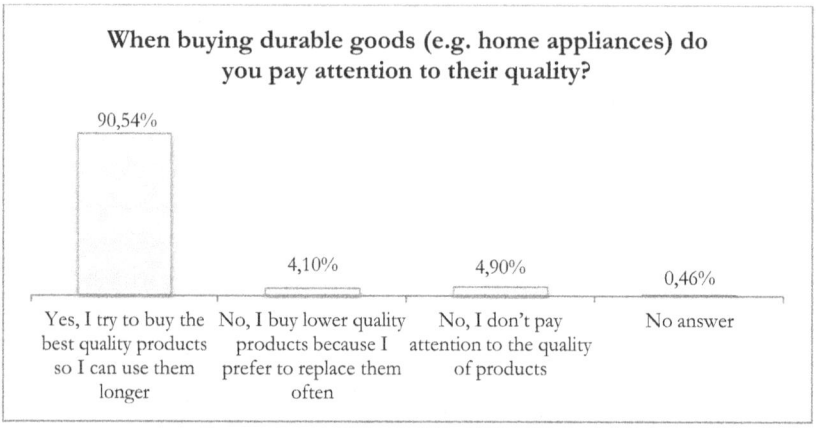

Fig. 8.6.4. Graphical representation of responses to question no. 6.

Figure 8.6.4. indicates that the respondents behave in a socially responsible way. One should also, however, take into account people's hedonistic nature which leads them to choose high quality durable goods so that they do not have to replace such products too often (saving) and so that they can derive pleasure from possessing goods which have higher subjective utility (i.e. more modern or designer products) than those which are available to others in their surroundings.

THE MODEL OF A HEDONISTIC HUMAN BEING VERSUS THE SOCIAL RESPONSIBILITY OF CONSUMERS

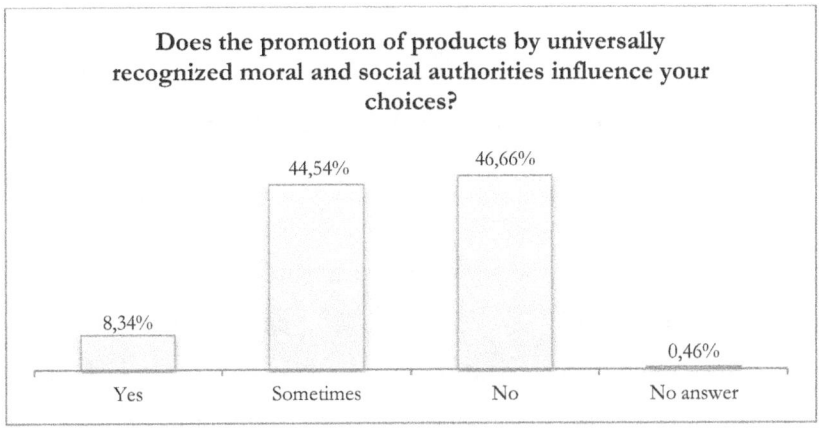

Fig. 8.6.5. Graphical representation of responses to question no. 7.

Figure 8.6.5 shows that society does not have much confidence in moral and social authorities. This most probably results from the fact that we believe that such authorities are motivated by self-interest (benefits), which additionally confirms that human behaviors are hedonistic in character.

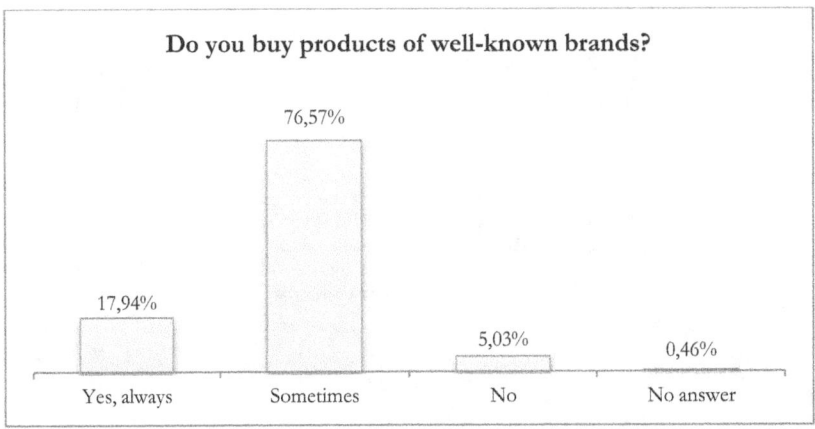

Fig. 8.6.6. Graphical representation of responses to question no. 9.

Analysis of the answers to question no. 9 cannot yield unambiguous results because these answers are influenced by the distribution of wealth among the respondents. On the other hand, it is possible to explain the fact that such a low percentage (18%) of respondents purchase products of well-known brands because they do not believe in the high quality of all famous brands. Moreover, the respondents probably often feel that the high prices of branded goods are unacceptable when compared to the prices of substitute goods. An analysis of the answers to question no. 10, which is connected with question no. 9, reveals the Veblen paradox, i.e. snobbish consumer behaviors, which also confirms that the model of a human being that has been adopted here is correct. And this explains the answers "because I can afford it" and "because it makes me feel better".

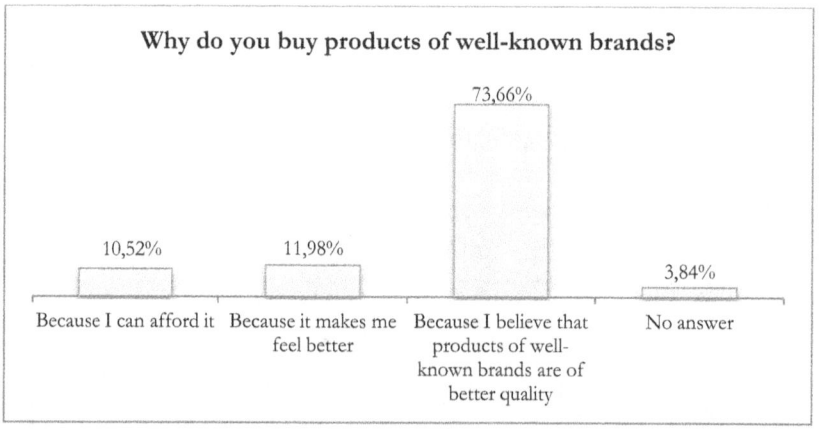

Fig. 8.6.7. Graphical representation of responses to question no. 10.

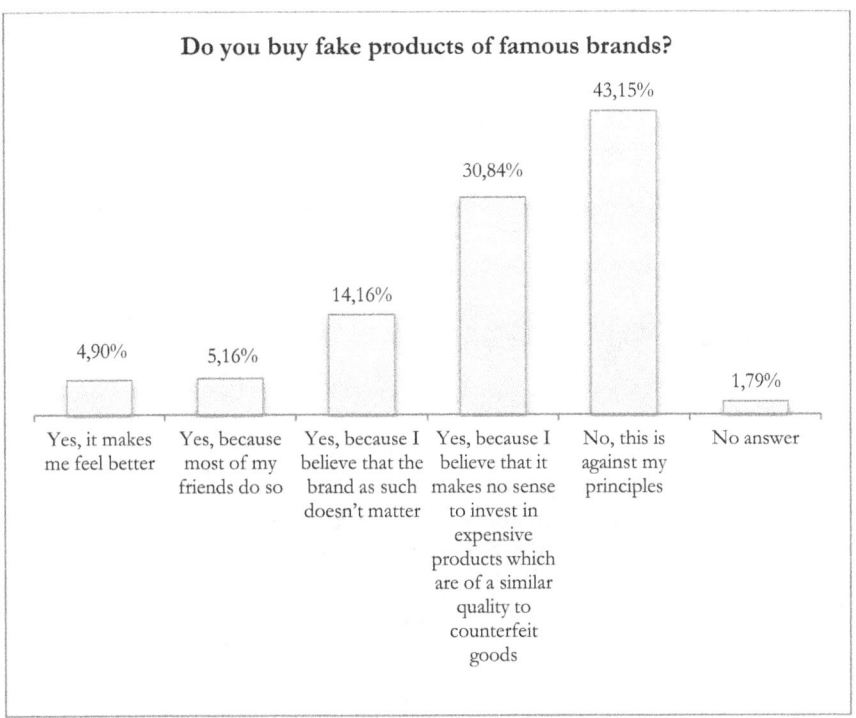

Fig. 8.6.8. Graphical representation of responses to question no. 11.

The answers to question no. 11 also indicate that human nature is hedonistic. This explains why only 43% of respondents answered "no, this is against my principles". The majority of the respondents subjectively rationalized their behaviors and, in accordance with the psychodynamic theory of a human being, tried to morally cleanse themselves of unethical and illegal actions.

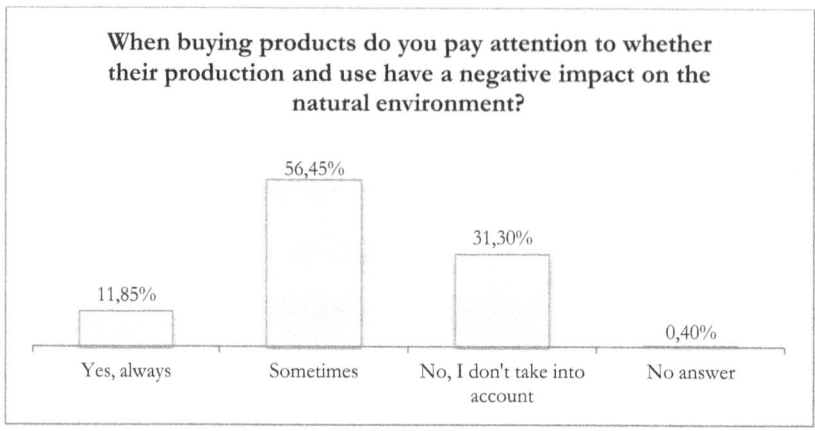

Fig. 8.6.9. Graphical representation of responses to question no. 12.

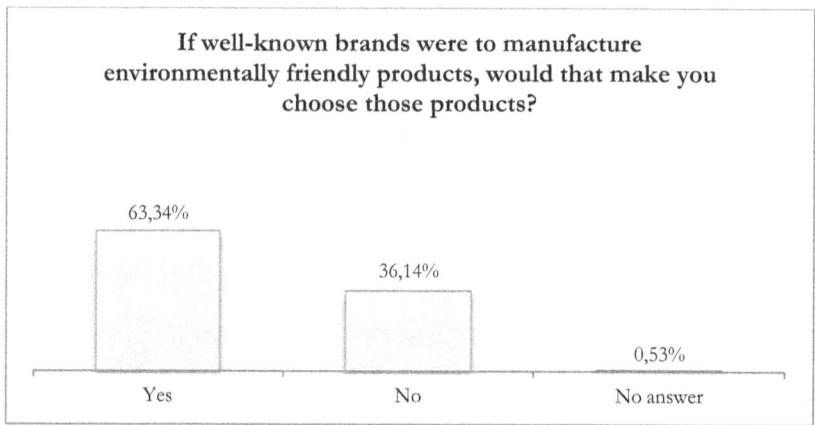

Fig. 8.6.10. Graphical representation of responses to question no. 13.

The responses to questions no. 12 and no. 13 are somewhat correlated. When giving answers to both of these questions, over 30% of respondents showed that protection of the natural environment was not important to them at all. This certainly means that the level of ecological and social responsibility in the group is low. In addition, the answers solely to question 12 indicate that only slightly more than 11% of respondents declare that they always buy environmentally friendly products. This further confirms that the level of ConSR is low.

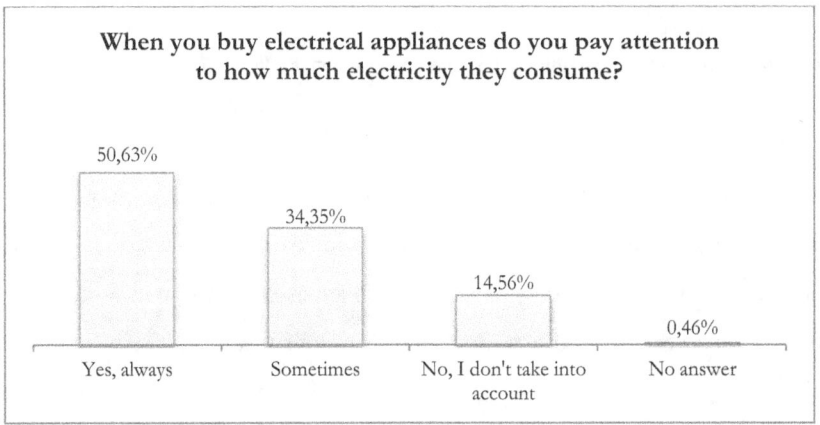

Fig. 8.6.11. Graphical representation of responses to question no. 14.

As for question 14, the answers show a lack of social responsibility among consumers, of whom only 50% declare that they buy energy-efficient appliances even though they can potentially benefit from saving electricity.

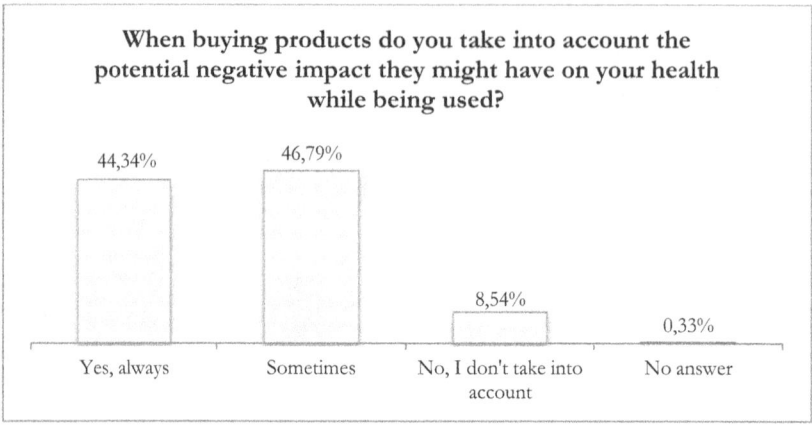

Fig. 8.6.12. Graphical representation of responses to question no. 15.

The responses to question 15 show the participants' high aversion to the risk of losing their health (hedonistic attitude), which is why only 8% of them gave answers indicating that they do not pay attention to the negative influence that certain products might have on their health.

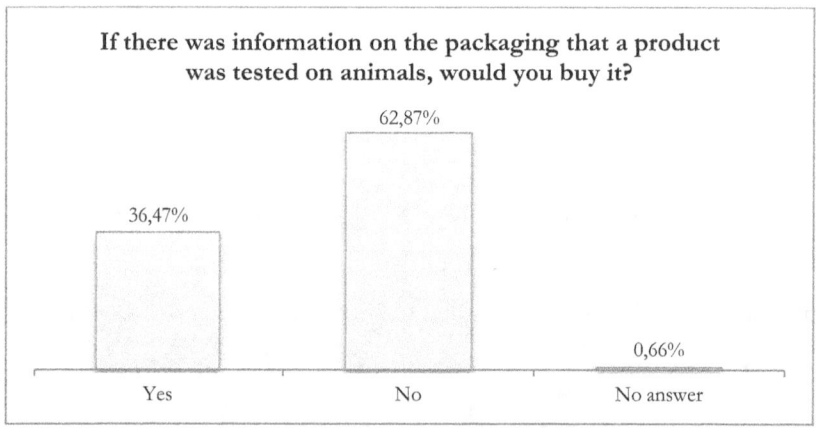

Fig. 8.6.13. Graphical representation of responses to question no. 16.

The responses to question 16 further confirm the absence of ConSR, which is evidenced by as many as 36% of the answers indicating that for the respondents it is not important at all whether products were tested on animals.

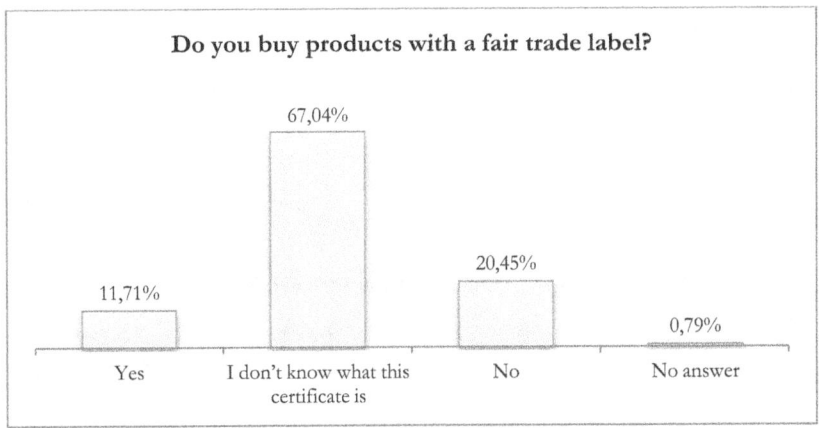

Fig. 8.6.14. Graphical representation of responses to question no. 19.

Figure 8.6.14 shows that there is another problem, i.e. the participants have very little knowledge concerning ecology and most of them do not know anything about certificates for products that are manufactured in accordance with the principles of social responsibility – 67% of the respondents do not know what a fair trade certificate is.

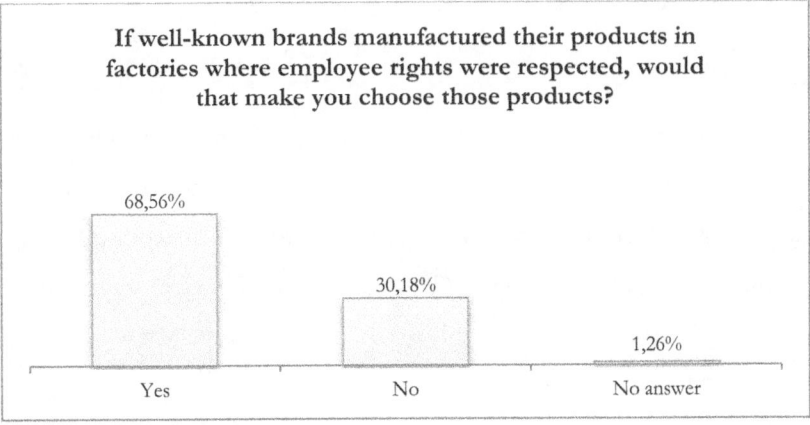

Fig.8.6.15. Graphical representation of responses to question no. 21.

As for the above question, one might expect that all of the respondents would answer "yes" – certainly none of them would like to work for a company which infringes on employee rights. Here too a low level of ConSR can explain this distribution of answers.

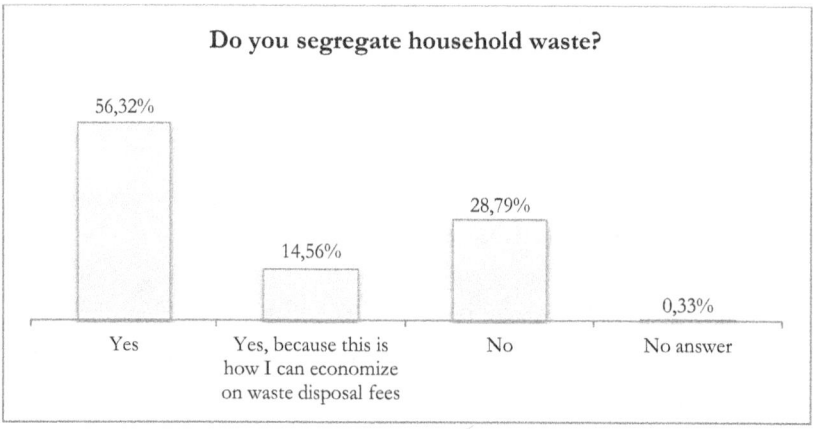

Fig. 8.6.16. Graphical representation of responses to question no. 22.

The responses to question no. 22 indicate that there are two problems. On the one hand, one can see that positive reinforcement leads to the desired behavior, which here amounts to segregating waste; on the other hand, a large number of the respondents (29%) are not bothered by the issue of environmental protection even if this would lead to financial gain.

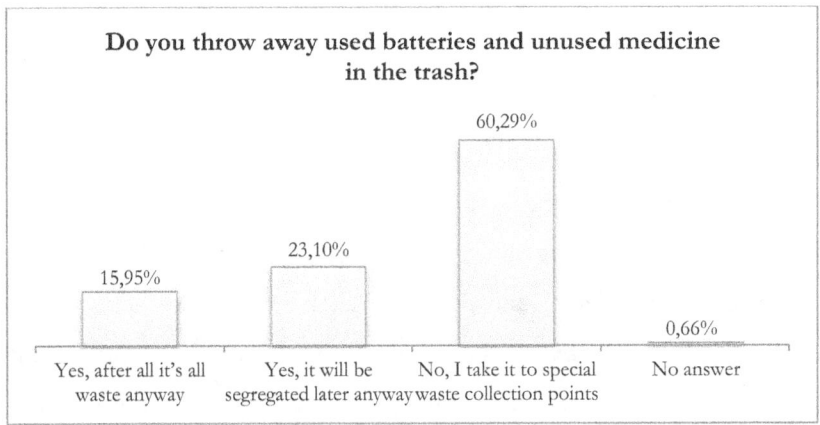

Fig. 8.6.17. Graphical representation of responses to question no. 23.

The answers to question 23 provide another example of low ecological awareness (knowledge). Nearly 40% of the respondents do not know how to deal with hazardous waste.

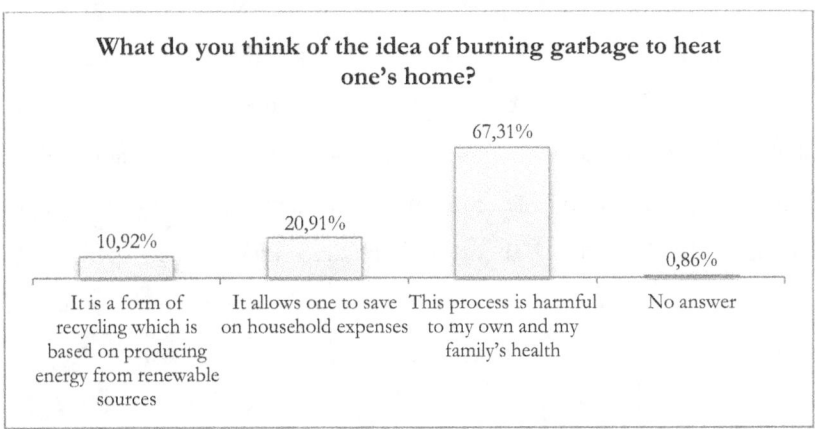

Fig. 8.6.18. Graphical representation of responses to question no. 24.

The answers to question no. 24 can be analyzed similarly to the answers to the previous question. A similar number of respondents knew nothing about the basic rules of environmental protection and waste disposal.

It can generally be concluded from the analysis of individual answers that the level of social responsibility in the studied community is low. What is more, the respondents' knowledge of ecology is unsatisfactory. The answers also point to the compatibility of consumer behaviors with the adopted model of a hedonistic human being. From the respondents' behaviors (as declared) it can be concluded that they are very often motivated by the prospect of obtaining a benefit (pleasure) or an aversion to the risk of experiencing unpleasantness.

The connection between the answers and the respondents' characteristics

Additionally, a cross-sectional analysis of the answers was carried out which showed that only one of the respondents' characteristics had a significant influence on the distribution of these answers, i.e. the monthly net income, which is disposable income. This additionally confirms that the level of affluence is an important determinant of socially responsible consumer behaviors. The impact of the other characteristics on the percentage distribution of the answers was small. The influence of the amount of income on the answers to selected questions is presented below.

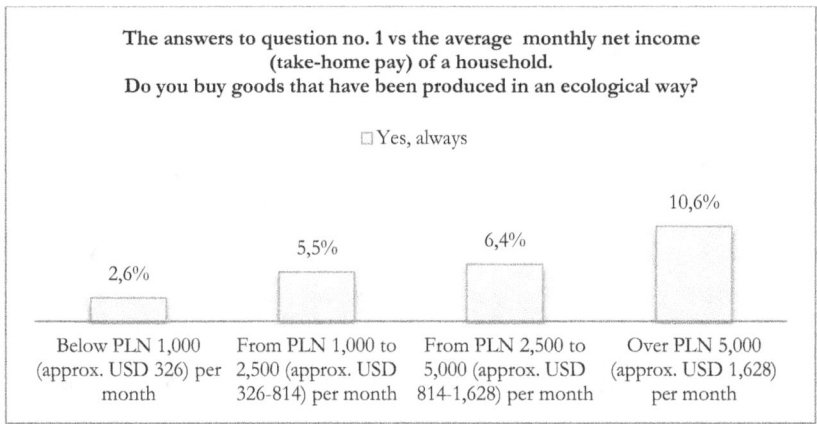

Fig. 8.6.19. Graphical representation of responses to question no. 1 broken down by income groups.

Figure 8.6.19 shows that there is a positive relationship between affluence and consumer social responsibility. There is even a more than fourfold difference in the level of responsible behaviors between the least and the most wealthy groups of respondents. If one assumes that well-known brands are more socially responsible, then the next chart (Fig. 8.6.20) indicates the same relationship. In addition, it can be stated that the distribution of the answers is not that wide, which can be ascribed to hedonistic human nature which here manifests itself as a desire to raise one's self-esteem (pleasure) and to impress others (pleasure) regardless of the level of one's income, which the answers presented in yet another chart (Fig. 8.6.21) show.

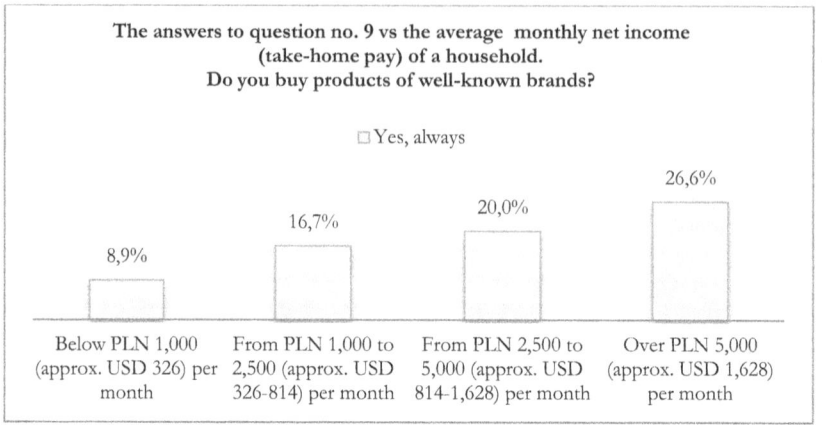

Fig. 8.6.20. Graphical representation of responses to question no. 9 broken down by income groups.

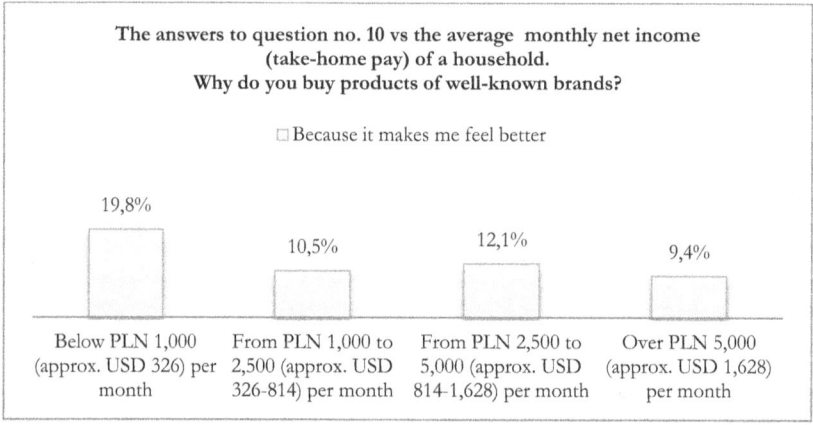

Fig. 8.6.21. Graphical representation of responses to question no. 10 broken down by income groups.

Figure 8.6.21 shows that twice as many people with a low income than those in the highest income group try to make themselves feel better by purchasing products of famous brands. This fact confirms that human nature is hedonistic and shows how the definitions of a benefit, or pleasure, change as the level of people's affluence grows.

THE MODEL OF A HEDONISTIC HUMAN BEING VERSUS THE SOCIAL RESPONSIBILITY OF CONSUMERS

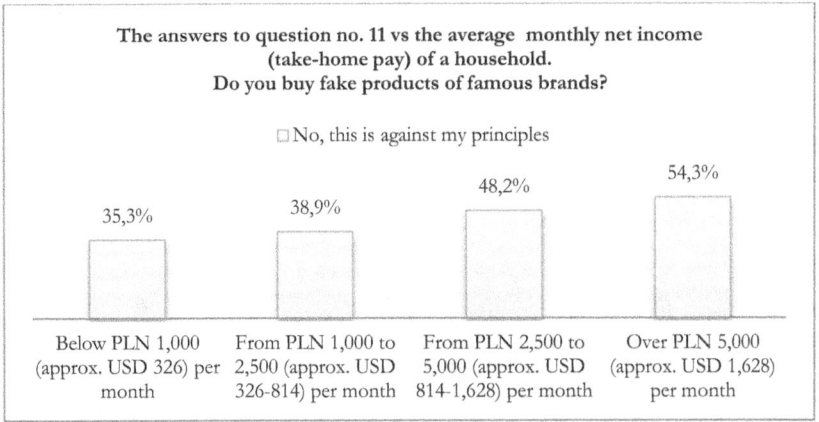

Fig. 8.6.22. Graphical representation of responses to question no. 11 broken down by income groups.

Both the chart below and the one above show the dependence of affluence and the level of ConSR, which clearly confirms the hypothesis that social responsibility emerges after one has achieved a particular level of wealthiness. In both cases the level of socially responsible behavior is nearly twice as high in the wealthiest group than in the group with the lowest income.

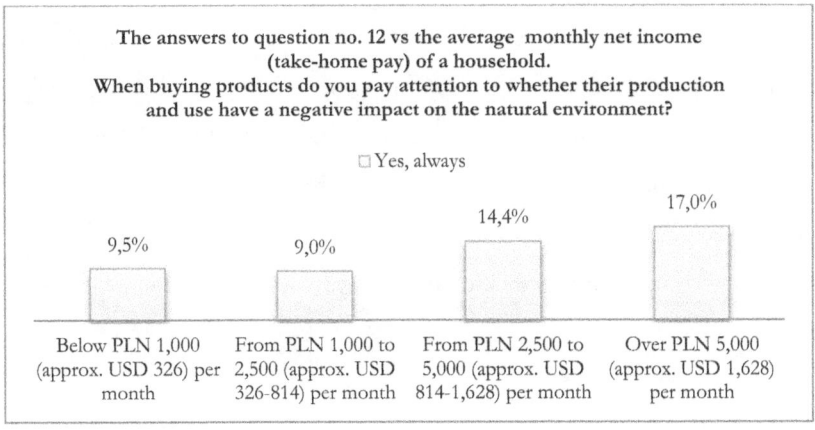

Fig. 8.6.23. Graphical representation of responses to question no. 12 broken down by income groups.

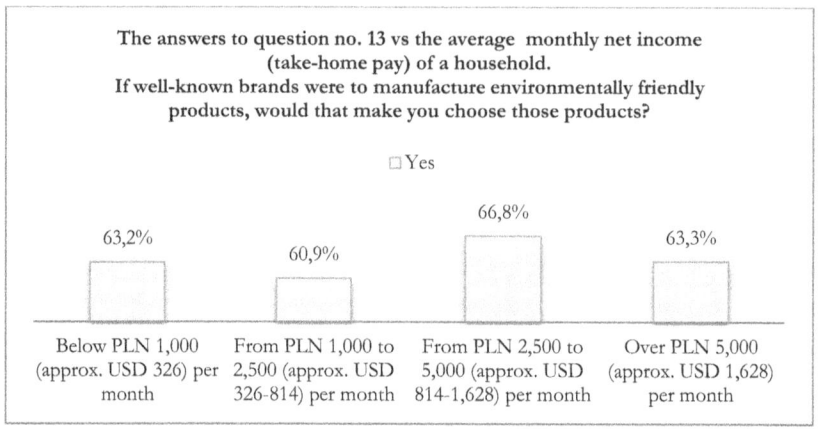

Fig. 8.6.24. Graphical representation of responses to question no. 13 broken down by income groups.

The two following charts indicate that the distribution of the answers among different income groups is almost identical. As for the first chart, there is the phenomenon of a person being used to a given brand (a habit) and the belief that well-known brands are more responsible. The second chart indicates that the level of an aversion to the risk of losing one's health (unpleasantness) is the same in all income groups, which further proves that the adopted concept of hedonistic human nature is correct.

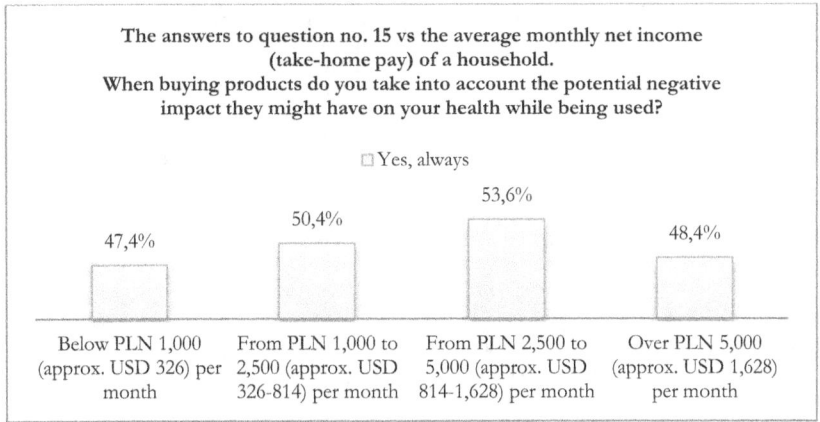

Fig. 8.6.25. Graphical representation of responses to question no. 15 broken down by income groups.

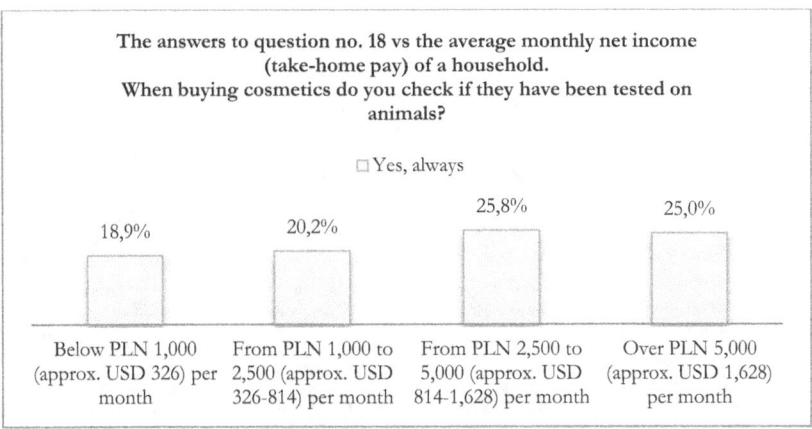

Fig. 8.6.26. Graphical representation of responses to question no. 18 broken down by income groups.

The influence of wealthiness on the level of ConSR can again be seen, both in the chart above and below, which show that these two factors are positively correlated.

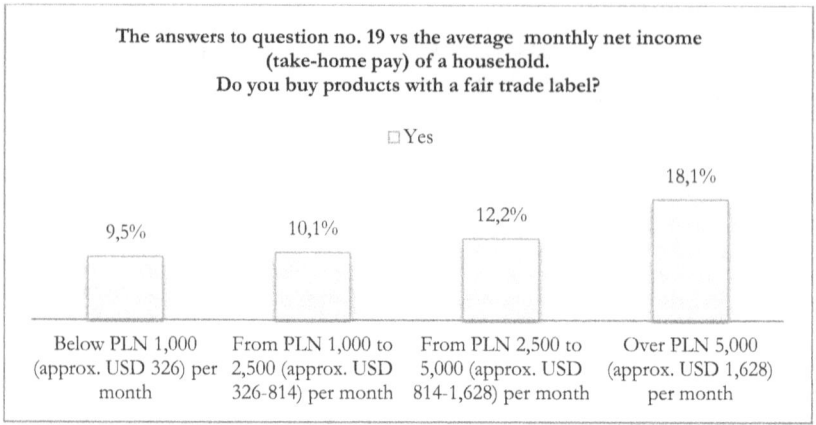

Fig. 8.6.27. Graphical representation of responses to question no. 19 broken down by income groups.

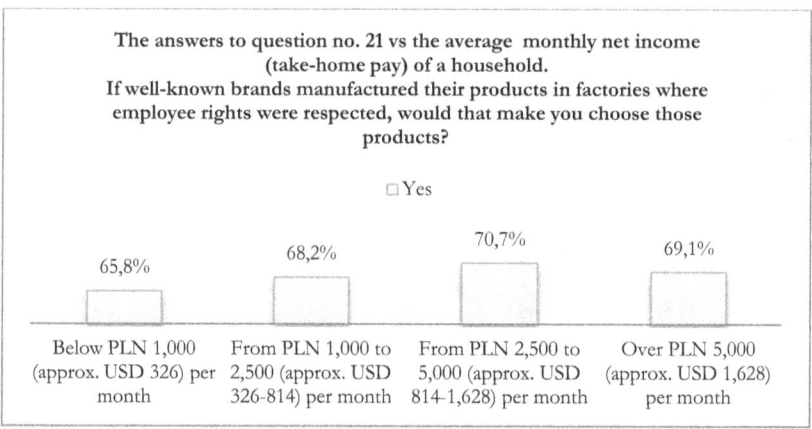

Fig. 8.6.28. Graphical representation of responses to question no. 21 broken down by income groups.

The last chart once again shows that there is a similar distribution of answers across all of the income groups, i.e. that the level of affluence does not have an influence on the answers that were provided by the respondents. These results can be ascribed to human nature, which here manifests itself in an aversion to the risk of being employed at an unethical company. We support the production of such goods because we subconsciously want to work for businesses that behave in an ethical way, thus the current level of one's income does not matter.

To sum up, the following three conclusions can definitely be drawn from this research study:

- The level of consumer social responsibility in Polish society is low.
- Affluence is an important factor determining the growth of the level of ConSR.
- Hedonistic human nature is manifested in consumer behaviors.

The results of this study are also important for constructing the possible scenario of the development of ConSR both in Poland and all over the world. As for Poland, it is the current level of knowledge and socially responsible behavior that are important, whereas globally it is the answers that confirm the correctness of the adopted model of *Homo hedonismus* that are significant. Only if the proposed model of a human being is accepted and if human nature, as described by the model, is taken into account; i.e. if primarily positive reinforcement is used, can we expect that the level of ConSR will grow.

CHAPTER NINE

*

Prospects for the development of ConSR

Given the current development of CSR and socially responsible behaviors, one can hardly be optimistic and believe that people have a chance for a future in which most businesses and consumers will truly be socially responsible. Judging from a human being's hedonistic nature, there is no reason to assume that people will suddenly become both socially and ecologically responsible without being positively motivated. The same is true for businesses, which are also based on organized social structures. It is the people or teams that decide about an organization's strategy; therefore, one can hardly assume that companies will not follow the principles of hedonism. Previous experiences show that the concept of CSR is most often used as a PR slogan and it does not constitute a real strategy that would be implemented in all areas of business activity. How else could one interpret, for example, the behavior of many financial institutions which issue nice and neat reports on CSR but which do not inform consumers about the real parameters of their products in everyday marketing practice. It is most probable that everyone has encountered advertisements for bank loans with an interest rate of, for example 6.99%, while the real interest rate was over 20%. The production of dietary supplements, i.e. omega-3 fatty acid capsules, is another example of such practice. Among the largest producers of these supplements are "very responsible" companies from Scandinavia. None of them, however, is willing to announce the fact that they have located their factories in Peru where no principles of environmental protection are adhered to and where employees' rights are violated.

The behavior of consumers is no better. As was shown in the chapter dealing with the intention-behavior gap, 30% of the population wants to be socially responsible, but only 3% of people actually act according to their intentions. A simple walk through a supermarket and a look at the store's products will show what tendencies are prevalent in a given society. How many of these products carry labels with information about them being produced in a socially responsible way? And if the supply is low, does this not mean that there is no demand for such products?

Also, the highly uneven distribution of income in the world dashes hopes of rapid development of socially responsible consumer behaviors. C. K. Prahalad and A. Hammond [2007, pp. 7-34] pointed out that 65% of the world's population, i.e. 4 billion people, earned less than USD 2,000 a year. Moreover, the much needed growth of socially responsible investment that is needed in those parts of the world where the above-mentioned social groups live is yet to be seen.

According to the model of hedonistic human nature which has been introduced here, the human being seeks to obtain a benefit, i.e. pleasure, and has an aversion to unpleasant experiences. If governments do not make any changes in their countries' legal systems in order to introduce benefits for socially responsible consumer behaviors, then one will not be able to count on the aversion effect to produce the desired effect. Theoretically speaking, people might have an aversion to the possible contamination of the natural environment in the future and to an increase in the number of related social diseases, which would be an unpleasant experience. Unfortunately, if people do not know exactly when an unpleasant event will occur, then they will usually not be afraid of such future experiences. In addition, given that many entrepreneurs are having their factories built in locations that are far away from where their capital comes from and that they are destroying the natural environment in such places with impunity, one can hardly expect quick changes. Can we then expect more from others if corporations continue to act in this way and pretend that environmental contamination in places which are far away from their headquarters does not have any impact on the quality of their lives? We are all witnessing climate change and yet we are all silent – we do not want to point to its causes. For now this is pure hedonism and a desire to multiply wealth that is taking precedence.

Is this the only possible scenario? Certainly not, but this lack of optimism should not come as a surprise. People are the way they are and they do not change suddenly. Our nature has been shaped for over thousands or perhaps even millions of years of evolution. Does this make us bad? No. One may even put forward a hypothesis that if we were not hedonists, we might not be the dominant species on earth now. However, it might be beneficial if we acknowledged that this is who we are. Being aware of our true nature can only help us design any potential changes. Only if we know how to make a difference do we have the chance of introducing some changes. If we remain in this fallacy then we most certainly will not make it.

Summary

The proposed model of a hedonistic human being was developed based on an analysis of different economic theories that, in recent years, have challenged the model of *Homo economicus*, which is still being used in economics. In addition, various examples of consumer behaviors that are inconsistent with the model of *Homo economicus* have been taken into account; these were obtained based on my own research as well as my business experiences. I believe that the objectives which were formulated at the beginning have been fulfilled; and the proposed, i.e. the following, hypotheses have been verified:

The Axiomatic Model of a Hedonistic Human Being correctly reflects the real nature of human behavior

AMHHB is consistent with the economic theories of consumer behavior

AMHHB is consistent with the eclecticism of contemporary psychological conceptions of humankind, in particular with commonly accepted theories

The adopted method of verifying the correctness of the model of a hedonistic human being is in line with the principles of logical positivism. It was assumed that the theories and hypotheses related to consumer behavior which are cited here are true; this assumption seems to be legitimate if only because many of such theories have been formulated by the laureates of the Nobel Prize in Economic Sciences. Then the adopted model of a human being was checked for its compatibility with these theories. Because AMHHB proved to be consistent with the theories, this provided grounds for regarding this model as correct and consistent with actual consumer behaviors. The model's consistency with contemporary psychological conceptions of humankind was verified in a similar manner. Again, the fact that this model has proved to be consistent with many theories deriving from different concepts of the human being indicates that it is correct.

However, not everyone has to accept this reasoning as sufficient, thus it is proposed that the model be additionally tested for its consistency with the principles of the logic of scientific discovery as introduced by Karl Popper. According to Popper, one should point to an experiment that could falsify a given theory if one wants to prove that it is a scientific theory. He assumed that every theory which is scientifically correct must be theoretically falsifiable by means of a scientific experiment. As for the model of *Homo hedonismus*, it is proposed that the following experiment be used to falsify it:

100 people are randomly chosen and asked to buy some products in a supermarket for PLN 500 (approx. USD 163). Their task is to choose products that will allow them to function (survive) for a week. Each person should select products individually so that he or she does not know what products the other participants in the experiment are choosing.

According to the adopted axioms of AMHHB, every human being seeks to achieve a subjective benefit (utility) and to achieve its maximum amount, and every human being has his or her own subjective definition of a benefit, i.e. pleasure. This can be concluded from, for example, the two following axioms of AMHHB:

- *Homo hedonismus* seeks to achieve subjective pleasure, or a benefit, and to achieve its maximum amount, as subjectively perceived.
- Every *Homo hedonismus* might individually arrive at his or her own subjective definition of pleasure and a benefit, which may change during his or her lifetime due to the influence of the environment.

In view of how a hedonistic human being's nature has been defined it should be assumed that this model will be correct if there are no identical sets of purchased products. Otherwise, the model will be false. In fact, this model would be falsified in its entirety only if all of the participants chose the same sets of products. Therefore, AMHHB was proven to be a scientific model because an experiment that could potentially falsify it was indicated.

The proposed hypotheses are further confirmed by the results of the survey research which is presented in the previous chapter; an analysis of these results confirms that human beings possess a hedonistic nature.

If one accepts the axiomatics of the proposed model of a human being as being correct, then one can implement modified rules for influencing human behavior which may be more effective than those which were used until recently. This is particularly true of phenomena such as consumer social responsibility, sustainable development or corporate social responsibility. If we still have not succeeded in putting these ideas into practice then perhaps the time has come to change our way of thinking and to adopt new paradigms.

According to Thomas Kuhn, knowledge progresses stepwise and in a revolutionary manner by periodically undergoing paradigm shifts. Economists have accepted many laws and theories that contradict the idea of *Homo economicus*. Therefore, maybe it is time for another revolution? Perhaps this is the right moment to change the paradigm of human nature into one of *Homo hedonismus*?

At the same time it should be emphasized that the adopted model of a hedonistic human being correctly reflects the real mechanisms of consumer decisions but it does not represent the entirety of human nature. Introducing this model does not exclude the possibility of designing other models that would be more complete and would serve a different purpose.

As has already been mentioned, this model does not take into account such psychological phenomena as feelings.

I am fully aware that the proposed model of a human being may seem controversial to many researchers. Some will certainly say that the human being is not a hedonist by nature. If the proposed hypotheses were accepted, this would mean that many theories in the fields of management science, economics, and psychology would have to be revised. Are we ready for this? Also, are we ready to admit that our nature is hedonistic?

These questions will remain unanswered for some time. However, I hope we will soon hear that the new model of *Homo hedonismus* has been positively received by the world of science.

Has the question which was raised in the introduction as to who rules the market been answered? Yes and no. It is difficult to give an unequivocal answer to this question. It can be concluded from the discussion that businesses are often able to evoke in us the desire to have certain products and sell almost everything to us by using various psychological techniques. On the other hand, it turns out that we are not simply at the mercy of our unconscious bodily reactions because we often make conscious consumer decisions.

References

- Adamczyk, J., 2009, *Społeczna odpowiedzialność przedsiębiorstw*, PWE, Warszawa.
- Akerlof, G. A., 1970, "The market for 'lemons': Quality uncertainty and the market mechanism", *The Quarterly Journal of Economics*, vol. 84, no. 3, pp. 488-500.
- Arvola, A., Vassallo, M., Dean, M., Lampila, P., Saba, A., Lahteenmaki, R., Shepherd, R., 2008, "Predicting intentions to purchase organic food: The role of affective and moral attitudes in the Theory of Planned Behavior", *Appetite*, vol. 50, pp. 443-454.
- Auger, P., Devinney, T. M., 2007, "Do What Consumers Say Matter? The Misalignment of Preferences with Unconstrained Ethical Intentions", *Journal of Business Ethics*, vol. 76, pp. 361-383.
- Balicki W., 2002, *Wykłady z metodologii nauk ekonomicznych*, WWSB, Poznań
- Belk, R., 1975, "Situational Variables and Consumer Behavior", *Journal of Consumer Research*, vol. 2, pp. 157-164.
- Bennis, W., Goleman, D., O'Toole, J., 2009, *Przejrzystość w biznesie*, MT Biznes, Warszawa.
- Bray, J., Johns, N., Kilburn, D., 2011, "An exploratory study into the factors impeding ethical consumption", *Journal of Business Ethics*, vol. 98, issue 4, pp. 597-618, DOI: 10.1007/s10551-010-0640-9 [accessed on October 17, 2013].
- Brinkmann, J., Peattie, K., 2008, "Consumer Ethics Research: Reframing the Debate about Consumption for Good", *EJBO Electronic Journal of Business Ethics and Organization Studies*, vol. 13, no. 1, pp. 22-31.

- Carrigan, M., Attalla, A., 2001, 'The myth of the ethical consumer – do ethics matter in purchase behavior?", *Journal of Consumer Marketing*, vol. 18, issue 7, pp. 560-577.
- Carrington, M., Neville, B. A, Whitwell, G. J., 2010, "Why Ethical Consumers Don't Walk Their Talk: Towards a Framework for Understanding the Gap between the Ethical Purchase Intentions and Actual Buying Behavior of Ethically-Minded Consumers", *Journal of Business Ethics*, vol. 97, pp. 139-158.
- Carrington, M., Neville, B. A., Whitwell, G. J., 2012, 'Lost in Translation: Exploring the Ethical Consumer Intention-Behavior Gap", *Journal of Business Research*, vol. 67, issue 1, http://dx.doi.org/10.1016/j.jbusres.2012.09.022_[accessed on October 17, 2013].
- Chodyński, A., Jabłoński, A., Jabłoński, M., 2008, *Environmental Corporate Social Responsibility (ECSR) – koncepcja strategiczna budowy wartości firmy oparta na kryteriach ekologicznych*, Przegląd Organizacji, no. 3.
- Cialdini, R. B., 2007, *Wywieranie wpływu na ludzi. Teoria i praktyka*, Gdańskie Wydawnictwo Psychologiczne, Gdańsk.
- Clavin, B., Lewis, A., 2005, 'Focus Groups on Consumers' Ethical Beliefs", in: *The Ethical Consumer*, Harrison, R. (ed.), Newholm, T., Shaw, D., London, pp. 173-187.
- Cowe, R., Williams, S., 2000, 'Who are the Ethical Consumers?", *Ethical Consumerism Report*, Cooperative Bank, http://www.cooperativebank.co.uk/servlet/Satellite?c=Pageandcid=1139903089615andpagename=CoopBank%2FPage%2FtplPageStandard [accessed on October 17, 2013].

- Crane, A., McWilliams, A., Mattem, D., Moon, J., Stegel, D., 2009, *The Oxford Handbook of Corporate Social Responsibility*, Oxford University Press, New York.
- Cyfert, Sz., Hoppe, G., 2011, *Społeczna i ekologiczna odpowiedzialność konsumentów jako determinanta skutecznej implementacji CSR i ECSR*, Ekonomika i Organizacja Przedsiębiorstwa, no. 8, pp. 13-21.
- Devinney, T. M., 2010, "Using Market Segmentation Approaches to Understand the Green Consumer", http://papers.ssrn.com/sol3/papers.cfm?abstract_id=1633996 [accessed on October 17, 2013].
- Devinney, T. M., Auger, P., et al., 2010, *The Myth of the Ethical Consumer*, Cambridge University, Cambridge.
- Devinney, T. M., Auger, P., Eckhardt, G., 2012, "Can the Socially Responsible Consumer Be Mainstream?", http://dx.doi.org/10.2139/ssrn.2153784 [accessed on October 17, 2013].
- Devinney, T. M., Auger, P., Eckhard, G., Birtchnell, T., 2006, "The Other CSR: Consumer Social Responsibility", *Stanford Social Innovation Review*.
- Devitiis, B., D'Alessio, M., Maietta, O. W., 2008, "A comparative analysis of the purchase motivations of Fair Trade products: the impact of social capital", in: *12th Congress of the European Association of Agricultural Economists – EAAE*, pp. 1-14.
- Dudziński P., Gotowska M., Hoppe G., Jakubczak A., Karaszewski R., 2013, *Obiektywna metoda pomiaru poziomu społecznej i ekologicznej odpowiedzialności konsumentów (ConSR)*, Ekonomia i Środowisko, no. 3, pp. 272-291.

- Dudziński, P., Hoppe, G., Karaszewski, R., 2012, *Model matematyczny indywidualnej społecznej odpowiedzialności*, Prace Naukowe Uniwersytetu Ekonomicznego we Wrocławiu, no. 274, pp. 59-69.
- Duesenberry, J., 1952, *Income, Saving, and the Theory of Consumer Behavior*, Harvard University Press, Cambridge.
- Duhigg, Ch., 2012, *Siła nawyku*, PWN, Warszawa.
- Eckhardt, G. M., Belk, R., Devinney, T., 2010, 'Why don't consumers consume ethically?", *Journal of Consumer Behavior*, vol. 9, issue 6, pp. 426-436.
- Falkowski, A., Tyszka, T., 2009, *Psychologia zachowań konsumenckich*, Gdańskie Wydawnictwo Psychologiczne, Gdańsk.
- Freud, S., 2009, *Psychologia nieświadomości*, Wydawnictwo KR, Warszawa.
- Friedman, M., Friedman, R., 2006, *Wolny wybór*, Aspekt, Sosnowiec.
- Futerra, S. C. L., 2005, *The Rules of the Game: The Principles of Climate Change Communication*, Department for Environment, Food and Rural Affairs, London, UK.
- Gasiul, H., 2012, *Psychologia osobowości. Nurty, teorie, koncepcje*, Difin, Warszawa.
- Goleman, D., 2007, *Inteligencja emocjonalna*, Media Rodzina, Poznań.
- Goleman, D., 2009, *Inteligencja ekologiczna*, REBIS, Warszawa.
- Gustafson, J., 2007, *Czym jest społeczna odpowiedzialność biznesu?*, in: *Biznes*, vol. 1, *Zarządzanie firmą, część 1*, PWN, Warszawa.
- Hagemann, H., Hauff, M. von, 2010, *Nachhaltige Entwicklung, das neue Paradigma in der Ökonomie*, Metropolis, Magdeburg.
- Hall, C. S., Lindzey, G., Cambell, J. B., 2013, *Teorie osobowości*, PWN, Warszawa.
- Handy, Ch., 2007, *Jaki jest cel istnienia firm?*, in: *Społeczna odpowiedzialność przedsiębiorstw*, Helion, Gliwice.

- Hofstede, G., 1980, *Culture's Consequences: International Differences in Work-Related Values,* Sage Publications, Beverly Hills CA.
- Hofstede, G., 2001, *Culture's Consequences: Comparing Values, Behaviors, Institutions and Organizations Across Nations,* 2nd Edition, Sage Publications, Thousand Oaks CA.
- Hofstede, G., 2011, *Dimensionalizing Cultures: The Hofstede Model in Context,* Online Readings in Psychology and Culture, vol. 2, issue 1, http://dx.doi.org/10.9707/2307-0919.1014.
- Hofstede, G., Hofstede, G. J., 2007, *Kultury i organizacje,* PWE, Warszawa.
- Hofstede, G., Hofstede, G. J., Minkov, M., 2010, *Cultures and Organizations: Software of the Mind,* McGraw – Hill, New York.
- Hoppe, G., 2012, *Zrównoważony rozwój potrzebuje nowych zasad polityki gospodarczej,* Handel Wewnętrzny, July-August, vol. 1, pp. 36-45.
- Hoppe, G., 2013, *Determinanty rozpoczęcia się nowego cyklu innowacyjnego, nazwanego „zielonym cyklem",* Logistyka Odzysku, no. 4, pp. 12-16.
- Hoppe, G., Karaszewski, R., 2013, *Odpowiedzialna konsumpcja,* Logistyka Odzysku, no. 1, pp. 102-105.
- Hostyński, L., 1998, *Wartości utylitarne,* Wydawnictwo UMCS, Lublin.
- Hostyński, L., 2006, *Wartości w świecie konsumpcji,* Wydawnictwo UMCS, Lublin.
- Jäger, J., 2010, *Was verträgt unsere Erde noch ?,* Fischer, Frankfurt am Main.
- Jurek, M., Kornacka, D., 2000, *Aktualność teorii społecznej odpowiedzialności przedsiębiorstwa,* Przegląd Organizacji, no. 5.
- Karaszewski, R., Karwacka, M., Paluszek, A., 2011, *Społeczna odpowiedzialność biznesu, perspektywy i kierunki rozwoju,* Wydawnictwo Naukowe UMK, Toruń.

- Karsaklian, E., Fee, A., 2012, "Motivating consumers to buy ethical products: A framework of four universal motives", in: *ANZMAC 2012 Proceedings*.
- Kietliński, K., 2006, *Religijne determinanty działalności gospodarczej w perspektywie czterech wielkich religii: judaizmu, buddyzmu, chrześcijaństwa i islamu*, Nierówności Społeczne a Wzrost Gospodarczy, no. 8, pp. 43-59.
- Kollmuss, A., Agyeman, J., 2002, "Mind the Gap: why do people act environmentally and what are the barriers to pro-environmental behavior?", *Environmental Education Research*, vol. 8, issue 3, pp. 239-260.
- Kozielecki, J., 2000, *Koncepcje psychologiczne człowieka*, Wydawnictwo Akademickie Żak, Warszawa.
- Kozielecki, J. (ed.), 2009, *Nowe idee w psychologii*, Gdańskie Wydawnictwo Psychologiczne, Gdańsk.
- Loewenstein, G., Prelec, D., 1992, "Anomalies and Intertemporal Choice: Evidence and an Interpretation", *The Quarterly Journal of Economics*, May, pp. 573-597.
- Maslow, A., 1998, *Toward a Psychology of Being*, third ed., Wiley, New York.
- Miegel, M., 2011, *Wohlstand ohne Wachstum*, List, Berlin.
- Mises, L. von, 2008, *Vom Wert der besseren Ideen. Sechs Vorlesungen über Wirtschaft und Politik*, München.
- Mises, L. von, 2011, *Ludzkie działanie. Traktat o ekonomii*, Instytut Ludwiga von Misesa, Warszawa.
- Nicholls, A., Lee, N., 2006, 'Purchase Decision-Making in Fair Trade and the Ethical Purchase 'Gap': 'Is there a Fair Trade Twix?'", *Journal of Strategic Marketing*, vol. 14, issue 4, pp. 369-386.
- Norris, P., Inglehart, R., 2006, *Sacrum i profanum. Religia i polityka na świecie*, NOMOS, Kraków.

- Prahalad, C. K., Hammond, A., 2007, *Jak obsługiwać biednych i dobrze na tym zarabiać?*, in: *Społeczna odpowiedzialność przedsiębiorstw*, Helion, Gliwice.
- Priddat, B. P., 2011, *Konsumentenverantwortung durch Produkttransparenz? Über Geschmackbildung und Konsumstilländerungen*, in: Heidbrink, L., Schmidt, I., Ahaus, B. (eds), *Die Verantwortung des Konsumenten*, Frankfurt am Main.
- Reller, A., Holdinghausen, H., 2011, *Wir konsumieren uns zu Tode*, Westend, Frankfurt am Main.
- Rogall, H., 2009, *Nachhaltige Ökonomie. Ökonomische Theorie und Praxis einer nachhaltiger Entwicklung*, Metropolis, Magdeburg.
- Rok, B., 2013, *Podstawy odpowiedzialności społecznej w zarządzaniu*, Poltext, Warszawa.
- Rothschild, M., Stiglitz, J., 1976, "Equilibrium in competitive insurance markets: An essay on the economics of imperfect information", *The Quarterly Journal of Economics*, vol. 90, no. 4, pp. 629-649.
- Seidl, I., Zahrnt, A., 2010, *Postwachstumsgesellschaft – Konzepte für die Zukunft*, Metropolis, Magdeburg.
- Shaw, D., Shui, E., 2002, "An assessment of ethical obligation and self-identity in ethical consumer decision-making: a structural equation modeling approach", *International Journal of Consumer Studies*, vol. 26, issue 4, pp. 286-293.
- Simon, H. A., 1957, *Models of Man: Social and Rational*, New York.
- Spence, M., 1973, "Job market signaling", *The Quarterly Journal of Economics*, vol. 87, no. 3, pp. 355-374.
- Stengel, O., 2011, *Suffizienz. Die Konsumgesellschaft in der ökologischen Krise*, OEKOM, München.
- Stiglitz, J., 1975, "The theory of 'screening', education, and the distribution of income", *The American Economic Review*, vol. 65, no. 3, pp. 283-300.

- Sułkowski, Ł., 2012, *Epistemologia i metodologia zarządzania*, PWE, Warszawa.
- Surdyk, J., 2007, *CSR: więcej niż PR – dążenie do osiągnięcia długofalowej przewagi konkurencyjnej*, in: *Biznes*, vol. 1, *Zarządzanie firmą, część 1*, PWN, Warszawa.
- Szmigin, I., Carrigan, M., 2006, "Exploring the Dimensions of Ethical Consumption", *European Advances in Consumer Research*, vol. 7, pp. 608-613.
- Thaler, R., Sherfin, H., 1981, "An Economic Theory of Self-Control", *Journal of Political Economy*, vol. 89, no. 2, pp. 392-406.
- Tomaszewski, T., 1984, *Ślady i wzorce*, WSiP, Warszawa.
- Tversky, A., Kahneman, D., 1979, "The Prospect Theory: An analysis of decision under risk", *Econometrica*, vol. 47, pp. 263-291.
- Tversky, A., Kahneman, D., 1986, "Rational Choice and the Framing of Decisions", *Journal of Business*, vol. 59, no. 4, pp. 251-278.
- Tversky, A., Kahneman, D., 1991, "Loss Aversion in Riskless Choice: A Reference-Dependent Model", *The Quarterly Journal of Economics*, vol. 106, no. 4, pp. 1039-1061.
- Vermeir, I., Verbeke, W., 2007, "Sustainable food consumption among young adults in Belgium: Theory of Planned Behavior and the role of confidence and values", *Ecological Economics*, vol. 64, pp. 542-553.
- Weizsäcker, E. U., Hargroves, K., Smith, M., 2010, *Faktor fünf. Die Formel für nachhaltiges Wachstum*, Droemer, München.
- Welzer, H., Wiegandt, K., 2011, *Perspektiven einer nachhaltiger Entwicklung*, Fischer, Frankfurt am Main.
- Wit, B. de, Meyer, R., 2007, *Synteza strategii*, PWE, Warszawa.

Annex 1

THE SURVEY QUESTIONNAIRE

Consumer Social Responsibility – ConSR

Greetings!

A research team under the supervision of Professor Robert Karaszewski, PhD, is carrying out research on the social responsibility of consumers and the factors that motivate consumers to choose particular products when they go shopping.

The study will be conducted in the first half of 2013.

This survey is anonymous and the results will be used solely for research purposes, therefore we ask that you provide us with sincere answers. The data we obtain will only be presented and analyzed in the aggregate.

The survey questionnaire consists of 31 questions and the estimated time for completion is about 15 minutes.

If you have any questions concerning this study, please contact Małgorzata Gotowska (PhD, Eng.) (tel. (52) 340-80-13, email: msrubkowska@utp.edu.pl) or Anna Jakubczak (PhD, Eng.) (tel. (52) 340-80-14, e-mail: ajakubczak@utp.edu.pl).

Instructions for completing the questionnaire: Please choose a statement that best describes your behavior when buying different kinds of goods by putting an "X" next to one of the answers (unless the instructions for a given question state otherwise).

I. Consumer decisions

1. Do you buy goods that have been produced in an ecological way?
   - ☐ Yes, always
   - ☐ Sometimes
   - ☐ No

2. Is there sufficient information about the products you purchase on the packaging?
   - ☐ Yes *(If you marked "Yes" please go to question no. 4)*
   - ☐ No

3. In your opinion, what kind of additional information is missing from labels on product packaging? *(Please mark up to three answers)*
   - ☐ Expiration date
   - ☐ Ingredients
   - ☐ How the product works
   - ☐ Instructions for use
   - ☐ The producer's name
   - ☐ Country of origin on the label
   - ☐ Eco-labels
   - ☐ GMO labels
   - ☐ Information on how much water was consumed per product unit during the production process
   - ☐ Information on a product's effects on one's health
   - ☐ The "Not tested on animals" label
   - ☐ Fair trade certificate

4. In your opinion, what information should labels on bread packaging contain? *(Please mark up to three answers)*

- ☐ Ingredients
- ☐ Expiration date
- ☐ The producer's name
- ☐ Country of origin on the label
- ☐ Eco-labels
- ☐ GMO labels
- ☐ Information on how much water was consumed per kilogram of product during the production process
- ☐ Information on a product's effects on one's health

5. When purchasing food products do you try to buy such an amount of food which will be entirely consumed?
    - ☐ Yes, always
    - ☐ Sometimes
    - ☐ No, I don't take this into account

6. When buying durable goods (e.g. home appliances) do you pay attention to their quality?
    - ☐ Yes, I try to buy the best quality products so I can use them longer.
    - ☐ No, I buy lower quality products because I prefer to replace them often.
    - ☐ No, I don't pay attention to the quality of products.

7. Does the promotion of products by universally recognized moral and social authorities influence your choices?
    - ☐ Yes, always *(If you marked "Yes" please go to question no. 9)*
    - ☐ Sometimes *(If you marked "Sometimes" please go to question no. 9)*
    - ☐ No

8. Why don't you take the opinions of universally recognized moral and social authorities into account when making consumer choices?
    - ☐ I only act according to my own beliefs

☐ I don't trust universally recognized authorities
☐ I think that universally recognized authorities promote products solely for personal gain

9. Do you buy products of well-known brands?
   ☐ Yes, always
   ☐ Sometimes
   ☐ No

10. Why do you buy products of well-known brands?
    ☐ Because I can afford it
    ☐ Because it makes me feel better
    ☐ Because I believe that products of well-known brands are of better quality

11. Do you buy fake products of famous brands?
    ☐ Yes, it makes me feel better
    ☐ Yes, because most of my friends do so
    ☐ Yes, because I believe that the brand as such doesn't matter
    ☐ Yes, because I believe that it makes no sense to invest in expensive products which are of a similar quality to counterfeit goods.
    ☐ No, this is against my principles

II. Natural environment and health

12. When buying products do you pay attention to whether their production and use have a negative impact on the natural environment?
    ☐ Yes, always
    ☐ Sometimes
    ☐ No, I don't take this into account

13. If well-known brands were to manufacture environmentally friendly products, would that make you choose those products?
    ☐ Yes
    ☐ No

14. When you buy electrical appliances do you pay attention to how much electricity they consume?
    ☐ Yes, always
    ☐ Sometimes
    ☐ No, I don't take this into account

15. When buying products do you take into account the potential negative impact they might have on your health while being used?
    ☐ Yes, always
    ☐ Sometimes
    ☐ No, I don't take this into account

16. If there was information on the packaging that a product was tested on animals, would you buy it?
    ☐ Yes
    ☐ No *(If you marked "No" please go to question no. 18)*

17. Why would you buy products that have been tested on animals?
    ☐ Because this is not important to me
    ☐ Because the product's price is affordable
    ☐ Because I wouldn't read this information
    ☐ Because this won't change anything

18. When buying cosmetics do you check if they have been tested on animals?
    ☐ Yes, always
    ☐ Sometimes
    ☐ No

III. Fair trade

19. Do you buy products with a fair trade label?
    - ☐ Yes *(If you marked "Yes" please go to question no. 21)*
    - ☐ No
    - ☐ I don't know what this certificate is *(If you marked "Yes" please go to question no. 21)*

20. Why don't you buy products with a fair trade label?
    - ☐ Because they're too expensive
    - ☐ Because I can't find them in the store where I do my shopping
    - ☐ I think this won't change anything

21. If well-known brands manufactured their products in factories where employee rights were respected, would that make you choose those products?
    - ☐ Yes
    - ☐ No

IV. Segregating waste

22. Do you segregate household waste?
    - ☐ Yes
    - ☐ Yes, because this is how I can economize on waste disposal fees
    - ☐ No

23. Do you throw away used batteries and unused medicine in the trash?
    - ☐ Yes, after all it's all waste anyway
    - ☐ Yes, it will be segregated later anyway
    - ☐ No, I take it to special waste collection points

24. What do you think of the idea of burning garbage to heat one's home?
    - ☐ It is a form of recycling which is based on producing energy from renewable sources
    - ☐ It allows one to save on household expenses
    - ☐ This process is harmful to my own and my family's health

Personal data

1. Sex:
    - ☐ Female
    - ☐ Male

2. Please indicate your age group:
    - ☐ Under 18 years old
    - ☐ 18-30 years old
    - ☐ 31-45 years old
    - ☐ 46-65 years old
    - ☐ 66 years old and older

3. Education (completed):
    - ☐ Elementary school
    - ☐ Junior high school
    - ☐ Basic vocational school
    - ☐ High school
    - ☐ Higher education (including bachelor's and engineer's degrees)

4. Where do you live?
    - ☐ Town/city – multi-family residential buildings
    - ☐ Town/city – single-family buildings
    - ☐ Rural areas

5. Livelihood:
   - ☐ Student
   - ☐ Currently unemployed
   - ☐ Earned income
   - ☐ Income from retirement pension/other kinds of pension (disability)

6. How many people live in your household?
   - ☐ 1
   - ☐ 2
   - ☐ 3
   - ☐ 4
   - ☐ 5
   - ☐ Over 5

7. What is the average monthly net income (take-home pay) of your household?
   - ☐ Below PLN 1,000 (approx. USD 326) per month
   - ☐ From PLN 1,000 to 2,500 (approx. USD 326-814) per month
   - ☐ From PLN 2,500 to 5,000 (approx. USD 814-1,628) per month
   - ☐ Over PLN 5,000 (approx. USD 1,628) per month

Thank you for taking the time to fill out this questionnaire.

Abstract

The Model of a Hedonistic Human Being versus the Social Responsibility of Consumers

Homo economicus has long ceased to be the model of a human being that is in line with actual human behavior. This fact has been confirmed by studies that were carried out by Nobel Prize winners at the beginning of this century; J. Stiglitz, D. Kahneman, M. Spence, G. Akerlof, and V. Smith proved that people are neither rational nor objective and that their decisions are often guided by emotions and subjectivity. In order to fill in the existing gap in the research, the author introduces a new model of a human being. The author uses seven axioms to define the concept of a hedonistic human being (*Homo hedonismus*) which, in the author's opinion, correctly reflects people's consumer behavior. This model is verified by checking how it pertains to the basic economic laws of consumer behavior and to the most important psychological conceptions of humankind. Furthermore, the influences of religion and culture on human behavior are presented. The second part of this book deals with the social responsibility of consumers from the perspective of the proposed model of a human being. The book then defines factors determining the emergence and growth of consumers' social responsibility and presents its development prospects on a global scale.

www.ingramcontent.com/pod-product-compliance
Lightning Source LLC
Chambersburg PA
CBHW051802170526
45167CB00005B/1853